CHINESE NAMES, SURNA
LOCATIONS & ADDRESSES

中国大陆地址集

FUJIAN PROVINCE - PART 5

福建省

ZIYUE TANG

汤子玥

ACKNOWLEDGEMENT

I am deeply indebted to my friends and family members to support me throughout my life. Without their invaluable love and guidance, this work wouldn't have been possible.

Thank you

Ziyue Tang

汤子玥

PREFACE

The book introduces foreigner students to the Chinese names along with locations and addresses from the **Anhui** Province of China (中国安徽省). The book contains 150 entries (names, addresses) explained with simplified Chinese characters, pinyin and English.

Chinese names follow the standard convention where the given name is written after the surname. For example, in 王威 (Wang Wei), Wang is the surname, and Wei is the given name. Further, the surnames are generally made of one (王) or two characters (司马). Similarly, the given names are also made of either one or two characters. For example, 司马威 (Sima Wei) is a three character Chinese name suitable for men. 司马威威 is a four character Chinese name.

Chinese addresses are comprised of different administrative units that start with the largest geographic entity (country) and continue to the smallest entity (county, building names, room number). For example, a typical address in Nanjing city (capital of Jiangsu province) would look like 江苏省南京市清华路 28 栋 520 室 (Jiāngsū shěng nánjīng shì qīnghuá lù 28 dòng 520 shì; Room 520, Building 28, Qinghua Road, Nanjing City, Jiangsu Province).

CONTENTS

ACKNOWLEDGEMENT..2

PREFACE 3

CONTENTS 4

CHAPTER 1: NAME, SURNAME & ADDRESSES (1-30) 5

CHAPTER 2: NAME, SURNAME & ADDRESSES (31-60) 17

CHAPTER 3: NAME, SURNAME & ADDRESSES (61-90) 28

CHAPTER 4: NAME, SURNAME & ADDRESSES (91-120) 40

CHAPTER 5: NAME, SURNAME & ADDRESSES (121-150) 51

CHAPTER 1: NAME, SURNAME & ADDRESSES (1-30)

601。姓名: 阚庆国

住址（酒店）：福建省莆田市涵江区桥九路 788 号强全酒店（邮政编码：552651）。联系电话：41746565。电子邮箱：qbopz@mvjbloqp.biz.cn

Zhù zhǐ: Kàn Qìng Guó Fújiàn Shěng Pútián Shì Hánjiāng Qū Qiáo Jiǔ Lù 788 Hào Qiáng Quán Jiǔ Diàn (Yóuzhèng Biānmǎ：552651). Liánxì Diànhuà：41746565. Diànzǐ Yóuxiāng：qbopz@mvjbloqp.biz.cn

Qing Guo Kan, Qiang Quan Hotel, 788 Qiao Jiu Road, Hanjiang District, Putian, Fujian. Postal Code: 552651. Phone Number：41746565. E-mail：qbopz@mvjbloqp.biz.cn

602。姓名: 宣钊岐

住址（广场）：福建省泉州市惠安县成智路 784 号全计广场（邮政编码：944031）。联系电话：63710664。电子邮箱：pulgx@swunckdq.squares.cn

Zhù zhǐ: Xuān Zhāo Qí Fújiàn Shěng Quánzhōu Shì Huìānxiàn Chéng Zhì Lù 784 Hào Quán Jì Guǎng Chǎng (Yóuzhèng Biānmǎ：944031). Liánxì Diànhuà：63710664. Diànzǐ Yóuxiāng：pulgx@swunckdq.squares.cn

Zhao Qi Xuan, Quan Ji Square, 784 Cheng Zhi Road, Huian County, Quanzhou, Fujian. Postal Code: 944031. Phone Number：63710664. E-mail：pulgx@swunckdq.squares.cn

603。姓名: 司寇淹源

住址（广场）：福建省厦门市湖里区居翰路 212 号汉伦广场（邮政编码：655291）。联系电话：77744774。电子邮箱：svpgd@cisdeyhf.squares.cn

Zhù zhǐ: Sīkòu Yān Yuán Fújiàn Shěng Xiàmén Shì Hú Lǐ Qū Jū Hàn Lù 212 Hào Hàn Lún Guǎng Chǎng（Yóuzhèng Biānmǎ：655291）. Liánxì Diànhuà：77744774. Diànzǐ Yóuxiāng：svpgd@cisdeyhf.squares.cn

Yan Yuan Sikou, Han Lun Square, 212 Ju Han Road, Huli District, Xiamen, Fujian. Postal Code: 655291. Phone Number：77744774. E-mail：svpgd@cisdeyhf.squares.cn

604。姓名：于愈人

住址（医院）：福建省龙岩市新罗区浩嘉路 593 号涛圣医院（邮政编码：539770）。联系电话：87017628。电子邮箱：ujemg@fqgohtxr.health.cn

Zhù zhǐ: Yú Yù Rén Fújiàn Shěng Lóngyán Shì Xīn Luō Qū Hào Jiā Lù 593 Hào Tāo Shèng Yī Yuàn（Yóuzhèng Biānmǎ：539770）. Liánxì Diànhuà：87017628. Diànzǐ Yóuxiāng：ujemg@fqgohtxr.health.cn

Yu Ren Yu, Tao Sheng Hospital, 593 Hao Jia Road, Silla District, Longyan, Fujian. Postal Code: 539770. Phone Number：87017628. E-mail：ujemg@fqgohtxr.health.cn

605。姓名：郦强中

住址（火车站）：福建省泉州市晋江市易院路 576 号泉州站（邮政编码：283306）。联系电话：69995989。电子邮箱：zkrij@fzraxcnk.chr.cn

Zhù zhǐ: Lì Qiǎng Zhòng Fújiàn Shěng Quánzhōu Shì Jìnjiāng Shì Yì Yuàn Lù 576 Hào Quánzōu Zhàn（Yóuzhèng Biānmǎ：283306）. Liánxì Diànhuà：69995989. Diànzǐ Yóuxiāng：zkrij@fzraxcnk.chr.cn

Qiang Zhong Li, Quanzhou Railway Station, 576 Yi Yuan Road, Jinjiang City, Quanzhou, Fujian. Postal Code: 283306. Phone Number：69995989. E-mail：zkrij@fzraxcnk.chr.cn

606。姓名：蓬南世

住址（湖泊）：福建省龙岩市永定区游亮路 675 号近光湖（邮政编码：430268）。联系电话：12179186。电子邮箱：hfkjz@frsznvgx.lakes.cn

Zhù zhǐ: Péng Nán Shì Fújiàn Shěng Lóngyán Shì Yǒngdìng Qū Yóu Liàng Lù 675 Hào Jìn Guāng Hú (Yóuzhèng Biānmǎ：430268). Liánxì Diànhuà：12179186. Diànzǐ Yóuxiāng：hfkjz@frsznvgx.lakes.cn

Nan Shi Peng, Jin Guang Lake, 675 You Liang Road, Yongding District, Longyan, Fujian. Postal Code: 430268. Phone Number：12179186. E-mail：hfkjz@frsznvgx.lakes.cn

607。姓名: 惠守懂

住址（医院）：福建省漳州市诏安县大其路 300 号圣泽医院（邮政编码：116539）。联系电话：99065498。电子邮箱：cdlfs@vixzhekb.health.cn

Zhù zhǐ: Huì Shǒu Dǒng Fújiàn Shěng Zhāngzhōu Shì Zhào Ānxiàn Dà Qí Lù 300 Hào Shèng Zé Yī Yuàn (Yóuzhèng Biānmǎ：116539). Liánxì Diànhuà：99065498. Diànzǐ Yóuxiāng：cdlfs@vixzhekb.health.cn

Shou Dong Hui, Sheng Ze Hospital, 300 Da Qi Road, Zhaoan County, Zhangzhou, Fujian. Postal Code: 116539. Phone Number：99065498. E-mail：cdlfs@vixzhekb.health.cn

608。姓名: 长孙启风

住址（机场）：福建省南平市武夷山市成顺路 295 号南平先盛国际机场（邮政编码：587678）。联系电话：16407469。电子邮箱：fbylj@gfbnhwio.airports.cn

Zhù zhǐ: Zhǎngsūn Qǐ Fēng Fújiàn Shěng Nánpíng Shì Wǔyíshān Shì Chéng Shùn Lù 295 Hào Nánpíng Xiān Shèng Guó Jì Jī Chǎng (Yóuzhèng Biānmǎ：587678). Liánxì Diànhuà：16407469. Diànzǐ Yóuxiāng：fbylj@gfbnhwio.airports.cn

Qi Feng Zhangsun, Nanping Xian Sheng International Airport, 295 Cheng Shun Road, Wuyishan City, Nanping, Fujian. Postal Code: 587678. Phone Number：16407469. E-mail：fbylj@gfbnhwio.airports.cn

609。姓名: 柯洵宝

住址（家庭）：福建省漳州市华安县翰学路 281 号征亮公寓 23 层 274 室（邮政编码：747499）。联系电话：93774797。电子邮箱：kgbxt@gljmreds.cn

Zhù zhǐ: Kē Xún Bǎo Fújiàn Shěng Zhāngzhōu Shì Huáānxiàn Hàn Xué Lù 281 Hào Zhēng Liàng Gōng Yù 23 Céng 274 Shì (Yóuzhèng Biānmǎ：747499). Liánxì Diànhuà：93774797. Diànzǐ Yóuxiāng：kgbxt@gljmreds.cn

Xun Bao Ke, Room# 274, Floor# 23, Zheng Liang Apartment, 281 Han Xue Road, Huaan County, Zhangzhou, Fujian. Postal Code: 747499. Phone Number：93774797. E-mail：kgbxt@gljmreds.cn

610。姓名: 益计葆

住址（公园）：福建省宁德市周宁县征居路 540 号宝敬公园（邮政编码：811641）。联系电话：69411498。电子邮箱：vsdyb@nhltucgq.parks.cn

Zhù zhǐ: Yì Jì Bǎo Fújiàn Shěng Níngdé Shì Zhōu Níngxiàn Zhēng Jū Lù 540 Hào Bǎo Jìng Gōng Yuán (Yóuzhèng Biānmǎ：811641). Liánxì Diànhuà：69411498. Diànzǐ Yóuxiāng：vsdyb@nhltucgq.parks.cn

Ji Bao Yi, Bao Jing Park, 540 Zheng Ju Road, Zhouning County, Ningde, Fujian. Postal Code: 811641. Phone Number：69411498. E-mail：vsdyb@nhltucgq.parks.cn

611。姓名: 宇文腾进

住址（家庭）：福建省平潭综合实验区平潭县炯金路 299 号咚德公寓 45 层 815 室（邮政编码：927155）。联系电话：20336031。电子邮箱：kioqe@aubkfhdi.cn

Zhù zhǐ: Yǔwén Téng Jìn Fújiàn Shěng Píng Tán Zònghé Shíyàn Qū Píng Tán Xiàn Jiǒng Jīn Lù 299 Hào Dōng Dé Gōng Yù 45 Céng 815 Shì (Yóuzhèng Biānmǎ: 927155). Liánxì Diànhuà：20336031. Diànzǐ Yóuxiāng：kioqe@aubkfhdi.cn

Teng Jin Yuwen, Room# 815, Floor# 45, Dong De Apartment, 299 Jiong Jin Road, Pingtan County, Pingtan Comprehensive Experimental Area, Fujian. Postal Code: 927155. Phone Number：20336031. E-mail：kioqe@aubkfhdi.cn

612。姓名: 越坡德

住址（火车站）：福建省平潭综合实验区平潭县守盛路 229 号平潭综合实验区站（邮政编码：678648）。联系电话：63896304。电子邮箱：bfklv@tvxsjhoa.chr.cn

Zhù zhǐ: Yuè Pō Dé Fújiàn Shěng Píng Tán Zònghé Shíyàn Qū Píng Tán Xiàn Shǒu Chéng Lù 229 Hào Píng Tán Zòngé íyàn Qū Zhàn (Yóuzhèng Biānmǎ：678648). Liánxì Diànhuà：63896304. Diànzǐ Yóuxiāng：bfklv@tvxsjhoa.chr.cn

Po De Yue, Pingtan Comprehensive Experimental Area Railway Station, 229 Shou Cheng Road, Pingtan County, Pingtan Comprehensive Experimental Area, Fujian. Postal Code: 678648. Phone Number：63896304. E-mail：bfklv@tvxsjhoa.chr.cn

613。姓名: 颛孙伦食

住址（火车站）：福建省南平市顺昌县屹稼路 566 号南平站（邮政编码：188808）。联系电话：55260287。电子邮箱：hqose@lfdkhzap.chr.cn

Zhù zhǐ: Zhuānsūn Lún Sì Fújiàn Shěng Nánpíng Shì Shùn Chāng Xiàn Yì Jià Lù 566 Hào Nánpíng Zhàn (Yóuzhèng Biānmǎ：188808). Liánxì Diànhuà：55260287. Diànzǐ Yóuxiāng：hqose@lfdkhzap.chr.cn

Lun Si Zhuansun, Nanping Railway Station, 566 Yi Jia Road, Shunchang County, Nanping, Fujian. Postal Code: 188808. Phone Number：55260287. E-mail：hqose@lfdkhzap.chr.cn

614。姓名: 尚俊豪

住址（公共汽车站）：福建省莆田市涵江区员轼路 817 号九俊站（邮政编码：410334）。联系电话：67886197。电子邮箱：lhtou@xlgtroyb.transport.cn

Zhù zhǐ: Shàng Jùn Háo Fújiàn Shěng Pútián Shì Hánjiāng Qū Yuán Shì Lù 817 Hào Jiǔ Jùn Zhàn (Yóuzhèng Biānmǎ：410334). Liánxì Diànhuà：67886197. Diànzǐ Yóuxiāng：lhtou@xlgtroyb.transport.cn

Jun Hao Shang, Jiu Jun Bus Station, 817 Yuan Shi Road, Hanjiang District, Putian, Fujian. Postal Code: 410334. Phone Number：67886197. E-mail：lhtou@xlgtroyb.transport.cn

615。姓名: 蒋钦涛

住址（广场）：福建省泉州市惠安县毅葛路 698 号沛友广场（邮政编码：816082）。联系电话：61112215。电子邮箱：cpqad@hmbfgure.squares.cn

Zhù zhǐ: Jiǎng Qīn Tāo Fújiàn Shěng Quánzhōu Shì Huìānxiàn Yì Gé Lù 698 Hào Bèi Yǒu Guǎng Chǎng (Yóuzhèng Biānmǎ：816082). Liánxì Diànhuà：61112215. Diànzǐ Yóuxiāng：cpqad@hmbfgure.squares.cn

Qin Tao Jiang, Bei You Square, 698 Yi Ge Road, Huian County, Quanzhou, Fujian. Postal Code: 816082. Phone Number：61112215. E-mail：cpqad@hmbfgure.squares.cn

616。姓名: 贝翰波

住址（寺庙）：福建省三明市泰宁县骥仓路 564 号员亭寺（邮政编码：568058）。联系电话：95627777。电子邮箱：duwvj@blydmfvs.god.cn

Zhù zhǐ: Bèi Hàn Bō Fújiàn Shěng Sānmíng Shì Tài Níngxiàn Jì Cāng Lù 564 Hào Yún Tíng Sì (Yóuzhèng Biānmǎ：568058). Liánxì Diànhuà：95627777. Diànzǐ Yóuxiāng：duwvj@blydmfvs.god.cn

Han Bo Bei, Yun Ting Temple, 564 Ji Cang Road, Taining County, Sanming, Fujian. Postal Code: 568058. Phone Number：95627777. E-mail：duwvj@blydmfvs.god.cn

617。姓名: 宰坡骥

住址（博物院）：福建省宁德市古田县进涛路 599 号宁德博物馆（邮政编码：244866）。联系电话：44334586。电子邮箱：ewjko@qmposbiy.museums.cn

Zhù zhǐ: Zǎi Pō Jì Fújiàn Shěng Níngdé Shì Gǔtián Xiàn Jìn Tāo Lù 599 Hào Níngdé Bó Wù Guǎn（Yóuzhèng Biānmǎ：244866). Liánxì Diànhuà：44334586. Diànzǐ Yóuxiāng：ewjko@qmposbiy.museums.cn

Po Ji Zai, Ningde Museum, 599 Jin Tao Road, Gutian County, Ningde, Fujian. Postal Code: 244866. Phone Number：44334586. E-mail：ewjko@qmposbiy.museums.cn

618。姓名: 归舟惟

住址（酒店）：福建省漳州市漳浦县兵昌路 952 号山愈酒店（邮政编码：861410）。联系电话：34088530。电子邮箱：dziwx@ltosynxi.biz.cn

Zhù zhǐ: Guī Zhōu Wéi Fújiàn Shěng Zhāngzhōu Shì Zhāng Pǔ Xiàn Bīng Chāng Lù 952 Hào Shān Yù Jiǔ Diàn（Yóuzhèng Biānmǎ：861410). Liánxì Diànhuà：34088530. Diànzǐ Yóuxiāng：dziwx@ltosynxi.biz.cn

Zhou Wei Gui, Shan Yu Hotel, 952 Bing Chang Road, Zhangpu County, Zhangzhou, Fujian. Postal Code: 861410. Phone Number：34088530. E-mail：dziwx@ltosynxi.biz.cn

619。姓名: 郁舟大

住址（大学）：福建省福州市福清市福国大学楚际路 201 号（邮政编码：489253）。联系电话：65377571。电子邮箱：upojd@gijmvyrs.edu.cn

Zhù zhǐ: Yù Zhōu Dà Fújiàn Shěng Fúzhōu Shì Fúqīng Shì Fú Guó DàxuéChǔ Jì Lù 201 Hào（Yóuzhèng Biānmǎ：489253). Liánxì Diànhuà：65377571. Diànzǐ Yóuxiāng：upojd@gijmvyrs.edu.cn

Zhou Da Yu, Fu Guo University, 201 Chu Ji Road, Fuqing City, Fuzhou, Fujian. Postal Code: 489253. Phone Number：65377571. E-mail：upojd@gijmvyrs.edu.cn

620。姓名: 糜焯坡

住址（公共汽车站）：福建省三明市清流县珏克路 258 号兵石站（邮政编码：569090）。联系电话：47878091。电子邮箱：vaqnr@uwtjfzqs.transport.cn

Zhù zhǐ: Mí Chāo Pō Fújiàn Shěng Sānmíng Shì Qīngliú Xiàn Jué Kè Lù 258 Hào Bīng Shí Zhàn（Yóuzhèng Biānmǎ：569090). Liánxì Diànhuà：47878091. Diànzǐ Yóuxiāng：vaqnr@uwtjfzqs.transport.cn

Chao Po Mi, Bing Shi Bus Station, 258 Jue Ke Road, Qingliu County, Sanming, Fujian. Postal Code: 569090. Phone Number：47878091. E-mail：vaqnr@uwtjfzqs.transport.cn

621。姓名: 慎铁食

住址（大学）：福建省福州市闽侯县民智大学盛毅路 322 号（邮政编码：627737）。联系电话：28761167。电子邮箱：fpmjq@kanmzide.edu.cn

Zhù zhǐ: Shèn Tiě Yì Fújiàn Shěng Fúzhōu Shì Mǐn Hóu Xiàn Mín Zhì DàxuéChéng Yì Lù 322 Hào（Yóuzhèng Biānmǎ：627737). Liánxì Diànhuà：28761167. Diànzǐ Yóuxiāng：fpmjq@kanmzide.edu.cn

Tie Yi Shen, Min Zhi University, 322 Cheng Yi Road, Minhou County, Fuzhou, Fujian. Postal Code: 627737. Phone Number：28761167. E-mail：fpmjq@kanmzide.edu.cn

622。姓名: 禹黎圣

住址（机场）：福建省南平市武夷山市炯全路 900 号南平计译国际机场（邮政编码：892757）。联系电话：65285595。电子邮箱：eldfh@cpbwgyrz.airports.cn

Zhù zhǐ: Yǔ Lí Shèng Fújiàn Shěng Nánpíng Shì Wǔyíshān Shì Jiǒng Quán Lù 900 Hào Nánpíng Jì Yì Guó Jì Jī Chǎng（Yóuzhèng Biānmǎ：892757）. Liánxì Diànhuà：65285595. Diànzǐ Yóuxiāng：eldfh@cpbwgyrz.airports.cn

Li Sheng Yu, Nanping Ji Yi International Airport, 900 Jiong Quan Road, Wuyishan City, Nanping, Fujian. Postal Code: 892757. Phone Number：65285595. E-mail：eldfh@cpbwgyrz.airports.cn

623。姓名: 辛铁盛

住址（酒店）：福建省漳州市芗城区洵近路 469 号化土酒店（邮政编码：455367）。联系电话：43874010。电子邮箱：ftkmb@diwmbgpz.biz.cn

Zhù zhǐ: Xīn Tiě Chéng Fújiàn Shěng Zhāngzhōu Shì Xiāng Chéngqū Xún Jìn Lù 469 Hào Huà Tǔ Jiǔ Diàn（Yóuzhèng Biānmǎ：455367）. Liánxì Diànhuà：43874010. Diànzǐ Yóuxiāng：ftkmb@diwmbgpz.biz.cn

Tie Cheng Xin, Hua Tu Hotel, 469 Xun Jin Road, Xiangcheng District, Zhangzhou, Fujian. Postal Code: 455367. Phone Number：43874010. E-mail：ftkmb@diwmbgpz.biz.cn

624。姓名: 奚民强

住址（机场）：福建省南平市松溪县恩泽路 208 号南平振辉国际机场（邮政编码：464767）。联系电话：32276461。电子邮箱：lmevc@mwvteygo.airports.cn

Zhù zhǐ: Xī Mín Qiǎng Fújiàn Shěng Nánpíng Shì Sōng Xī Xiàn Ēn Zé Lù 208 Hào Nánpíng Zhèn Huī Guó Jì Jī Chǎng（Yóuzhèng Biānmǎ：464767）. Liánxì Diànhuà：32276461. Diànzǐ Yóuxiāng：lmevc@mwvteygo.airports.cn

Min Qiang Xi, Nanping Zhen Hui International Airport, 208 En Ze Road, Songxi County, Nanping, Fujian. Postal Code: 464767. Phone Number：32276461. E-mail：lmevc@mwvteygo.airports.cn

625。姓名: 邰柱智

住址（广场）：福建省漳州市诏安县盛屹路 176 号昌智广场（邮政编码：451110）。联系电话：65777075。电子邮箱：xhcpj@rnkpzafi.squares.cn

Zhù zhǐ: Tái Zhù Zhì Fújiàn Shěng Zhāngzhōu Shì Zhào Ānxiàn Chéng Yì Lù 176 Hào Chāng Zhì Guǎng Chǎng（Yóuzhèng Biānmǎ：451110). Liánxì Diànhuà：65777075. Diànzǐ Yóuxiāng：xhcpj@rnkpzafi.squares.cn

Zhu Zhi Tai, Chang Zhi Square, 176 Cheng Yi Road, Zhaoan County, Zhangzhou, Fujian. Postal Code: 451110. Phone Number：65777075. E-mail：xhcpj@rnkpzafi.squares.cn

626。姓名：滑渊勇

住址（公司）：福建省三明市尤溪县冠昌路 626 号惟帆有限公司（邮政编码：462998）。联系电话：38465394。电子邮箱：lwynu@eknwoibh.biz.cn

Zhù zhǐ: Huá Yuān Yǒng Fújiàn Shěng Sānmíng Shì Yóu Xī Xiàn Guān Chāng Lù 626 Hào Wéi Fān Yǒuxiàn Gōngsī（Yóuzhèng Biānmǎ：462998). Liánxì Diànhuà：38465394. Diànzǐ Yóuxiāng：lwynu@eknwoibh.biz.cn

Yuan Yong Hua, Wei Fan Corporation, 626 Guan Chang Road, Youxi County, Sanming, Fujian. Postal Code: 462998. Phone Number：38465394. E-mail：lwynu@eknwoibh.biz.cn

627。姓名：戎禹谢

住址（湖泊）：福建省南平市光泽县庆汉路 490 号居山湖（邮政编码：998222）。联系电话：66707454。电子邮箱：nrcgz@powrmngu.lakes.cn

Zhù zhǐ: Róng Yǔ Xiè Fújiàn Shěng Nánpíng Shì Guāngzé Xiàn Qìng Hàn Lù 490 Hào Jū Shān Hú（Yóuzhèng Biānmǎ：998222). Liánxì Diànhuà：66707454. Diànzǐ Yóuxiāng：nrcgz@powrmngu.lakes.cn

Yu Xie Rong, Ju Shan Lake, 490 Qing Han Road, Guangze County, Nanping, Fujian. Postal Code: 998222. Phone Number：66707454. E-mail：nrcgz@powrmngu.lakes.cn

628。姓名：虞庆人

住址（医院）：福建省平潭综合实验区平潭县己渊路 346 号强亭医院（邮政编码：477718）。联系电话：63667563。电子邮箱：rfuvb@wjxvzfpy.health.cn

Zhù zhǐ: Yú Qìng Rén Fújiàn Shěng Píng Tán Zònghé Shíyàn Qū Píng Tán Xiàn Jǐ Yuān Lù 346 Hào Qiáng Tíng Yī Yuàn (Yóuzhèng Biānmǎ：477718). Liánxì Diànhuà：63667563. Diànzǐ Yóuxiāng：rfuvb@wjxvzfpy.health.cn

Qing Ren Yu, Qiang Ting Hospital, 346 Ji Yuan Road, Pingtan County, Pingtan Comprehensive Experimental Area, Fujian. Postal Code: 477718. Phone Number：63667563. E-mail：rfuvb@wjxvzfpy.health.cn

629。姓名：甘翰毅

住址（大学）：福建省三明市将乐县寰征大学强学路 660 号（邮政编码：852474）。联系电话：21002836。电子邮箱：cndtv@oxuepsnk.edu.cn

Zhù zhǐ: Gān Hàn Yì Fújiàn Shěng Sānmíng Shì Jiāng Lè Xiàn Huán Zhēng DàxuéQiǎng Xué Lù 660 Hào (Yóuzhèng Biānmǎ：852474). Liánxì Diànhuà：21002836. Diànzǐ Yóuxiāng：cndtv@oxuepsnk.edu.cn

Han Yi Gan, Huan Zheng University, 660 Qiang Xue Road, Jiangle County, Sanming, Fujian. Postal Code: 852474. Phone Number：21002836. E-mail：cndtv@oxuepsnk.edu.cn

630。姓名：淳于光光

住址（医院）：福建省宁德市周宁县迅征路 788 号舟山医院（邮政编码：832694）。联系电话：24966134。电子邮箱：zyomj@byradizn.health.cn

Zhù zhǐ: Chúnyú Guāng Guāng Fújiàn Shěng Níngdé Shì Zhōu Níngxiàn Xùn Zhēng Lù 788 Hào Zhōu Shān Yī Yuàn (Yóuzhèng Biānmǎ：832694). Liánxì Diànhuà：24966134. Diànzǐ Yóuxiāng：zyomj@byradizn.health.cn

Guang Guang Chunyu, Zhou Shan Hospital, 788 Xun Zheng Road, Zhouning County, Ningde, Fujian. Postal Code: 832694. Phone Number：24966134. E-mail: zyomj@byradizn.health.cn

631。姓名: 汝腾化

住址（医院）：福建省莆田市涵江区红振路 911 号勇柱医院（邮政编码：804954）。联系电话：85016133。电子邮箱：qsxow@qgxphjwv.health.cn

Zhù zhǐ: Rǔ Téng Huà Fújiàn Shěng Pútián Shì Hánjiāng Qū Hóng Zhèn Lù 911 Hào Yǒng Zhù Yī Yuàn (Yóuzhèng Biānmǎ：804954). Liánxì Diànhuà：85016133. Diànzǐ Yóuxiāng：qsxow@qgxphjwv.health.cn

Teng Hua Ru, Yong Zhu Hospital, 911 Hong Zhen Road, Hanjiang District, Putian, Fujian. Postal Code: 804954. Phone Number：85016133. E-mail：qsxow@qgxphjwv.health.cn

632。姓名: 浦辉顺

住址（公司）：福建省宁德市福安市奎坤路 541 号顺歧有限公司（邮政编码：385614）。联系电话：25163386。电子邮箱：zdjvi@fasmqkoh.biz.cn

Zhù zhǐ: Pǔ Huī Shùn Fújiàn Shěng Níngdé Shì Fúān Shì Kuí Kūn Lù 541 Hào Shùn Qí Yǒuxiàn Gōngsī (Yóuzhèng Biānmǎ：385614). Liánxì Diànhuà：25163386. Diànzǐ Yóuxiāng：zdjvi@fasmqkoh.biz.cn

Hui Shun Pu, Shun Qi Corporation, 541 Kui Kun Road, Fuan, Ningde, Fujian. Postal Code: 385614. Phone Number：25163386. E-mail：zdjvi@fasmqkoh.biz.cn

633。姓名: 封乐绅

住址（医院）：福建省漳州市长泰区九胜路 939 号译尚医院（邮政编码：188153）。联系电话：53244550。电子邮箱：kbseu@sfrhgwyq.health.cn

Zhù zhǐ: Fēng Lè Shēn Fújiàn Shěng Zhāngzhōu Shì Zhǎng Tài Qū Jiǔ Shēng Lù 939 Hào Yì Shàng Yī Yuàn (Yóuzhèng Biānmǎ：188153). Liánxì Diànhuà：53244550. Diànzǐ Yóuxiāng：kbseu@sfrhgwyq.health.cn

Le Shen Feng, Yi Shang Hospital, 939 Jiu Sheng Road, Changtai District, Zhangzhou, Fujian. Postal Code: 188153. Phone Number：53244550. E-mail：kbseu@sfrhgwyq.health.cn

634。姓名：竺世己

住址（公共汽车站）：福建省龙岩市连城县秀炯路 689 号辉惟站（邮政编码：983472）。联系电话：82134095。电子邮箱：ehvly@byhmsqtr.transport.cn

Zhù zhǐ: Zhú Shì Jǐ Fújiàn Shěng Lóngyán Shì Liánchéng Xiàn Xiù Jiǒng Lù 689 Hào Huī Wéi Zhàn （Yóuzhèng Biānmǎ：983472). Liánxì Diànhuà：82134095. Diànzǐ Yóuxiāng：ehvly@byhmsqtr.transport.cn

Shi Ji Zhu, Hui Wei Bus Station, 689 Xiu Jiong Road, Liancheng County, Longyan, Fujian. Postal Code: 983472. Phone Number：82134095. E-mail：ehvly@byhmsqtr.transport.cn

635。姓名：盖白刚

住址（酒店）：福建省漳州市诏安县鸣红路 729 号乐沛酒店（邮政编码：919899）。联系电话：71322172。电子邮箱：fzguj@omykxdih.biz.cn

Zhù zhǐ: Gài Bái Gāng Fújiàn Shěng Zhāngzhōu Shì Zhào Ānxiàn Míng Hóng Lù 729 Hào Lè Pèi Jiǔ Diàn （Yóuzhèng Biānmǎ：919899). Liánxì Diànhuà：71322172. Diànzǐ Yóuxiāng：fzguj@omykxdih.biz.cn

Bai Gang Gai, Le Pei Hotel, 729 Ming Hong Road, Zhaoan County, Zhangzhou, Fujian. Postal Code: 919899. Phone Number：71322172. E-mail：fzguj@omykxdih.biz.cn

636。姓名：冉浩大

住址（湖泊）：福建省福州市台江区晗葆路 751 号刚克湖（邮政编码：160286）。联系电话：75892445。电子邮箱：hjuxp@arnqsogb.lakes.cn

Zhù zhǐ: Rǎn Hào Dà Fújiàn Shěng Fúzhōu Shì Tái Jiāng Qū Hán Bǎo Lù 751 Hào Gāng Kè Hú (Yóuzhèng Biānmǎ：160286). Liánxì Diànhuà：75892445. Diànzǐ Yóuxiāng：hjuxp@arnqsogb.lakes.cn

Hao Da Ran, Gang Ke Lake, 751 Han Bao Road, Taijiang District, Fuzhou, Fujian. Postal Code: 160286. Phone Number：75892445. E-mail：hjuxp@arnqsogb.lakes.cn

637。姓名: 傅友宝

住址（机场）：福建省平潭综合实验区平潭县屹员路 249 号平潭综合实验区臻超国际机场（邮政编码：904281）。联系电话：82761401。电子邮箱：katfy@zfvybcpq.airports.cn

Zhù zhǐ: Fù Yǒu Bǎo Fújiàn Shěng Píng Tán Zònghé Shíyàn Qū Píng Tán Xiàn Yì Yuán Lù 249 Hào Píng Tán Zòngé íyàn Qū Zhēn Chāo Guó Jì Jī Chǎng (Yóuzhèng Biānmǎ：904281). Liánxì Diànhuà：82761401. Diànzǐ Yóuxiāng：katfy@zfvybcpq.airports.cn

You Bao Fu, Pingtan Comprehensive Experimental Area Zhen Chao International Airport, 249 Yi Yuan Road, Pingtan County, Pingtan Comprehensive Experimental Area, Fujian. Postal Code: 904281. Phone Number：82761401. E-mail：katfy@zfvybcpq.airports.cn

638。姓名: 羿源岐

住址（公共汽车站）：福建省龙岩市连城县立桥路 489 号员庆站（邮政编码：634990）。联系电话：66018472。电子邮箱：hjuvb@vidxrmel.transport.cn

Zhù zhǐ: Yì Yuán Qí Fújiàn Shěng Lóngyán Shì Liánchéng Xiàn Lì Qiáo Lù 489 Hào Yuán Qìng Zhàn (Yóuzhèng Biānmǎ：634990). Liánxì Diànhuà：66018472. Diànzǐ Yóuxiāng：hjuvb@vidxrmel.transport.cn

Yuan Qi Yi, Yuan Qing Bus Station, 489 Li Qiao Road, Liancheng County, Longyan, Fujian. Postal Code: 634990. Phone Number：66018472. E-mail：hjuvb@vidxrmel.transport.cn

639。姓名: 商隆世

住址（家庭）：福建省南平市建瓯市炯柱路 625 号伦亮公寓 14 层 135 室（邮政编码：141890）。联系电话：70155281。电子邮箱：wckut@ntjkyhwe.cn

Zhù zhǐ: Shāng Lóng Shì Fújiàn Shěng Nánpíng Shì Jiàn Ōu Shì Jiǒng Zhù Lù 625 Hào Lún Liàng Gōng Yù 14 Céng 135 Shì (Yóuzhèng Biānmǎ：141890). Liánxì Diànhuà：70155281. Diànzǐ Yóuxiāng：wckut@ntjkyhwe.cn

Long Shi Shang, Room# 135, Floor# 14, Lun Liang Apartment, 625 Jiong Zhu Road, Jianou City, Nanping, Fujian. Postal Code: 141890. Phone Number：70155281. E-mail：wckut@ntjkyhwe.cn

640。姓名: 温毅其

住址（湖泊）：福建省平潭综合实验区平潭县腾威路 199 号舟强湖（邮政编码：427247）。联系电话：77521432。电子邮箱：kcazd@hlmboxgs.lakes.cn

Zhù zhǐ: Wēn Yì Qí Fújiàn Shěng Píng Tán Zònghé Shíyàn Qū Píng Tán Xiàn Téng Wēi Lù 199 Hào Zhōu Qiǎng Hú (Yóuzhèng Biānmǎ：427247). Liánxì Diànhuà：77521432. Diànzǐ Yóuxiāng：kcazd@hlmboxgs.lakes.cn

Yi Qi Wen, Zhou Qiang Lake, 199 Teng Wei Road, Pingtan County, Pingtan Comprehensive Experimental Area, Fujian. Postal Code: 427247. Phone Number：77521432. E-mail：kcazd@hlmboxgs.lakes.cn

641。姓名: 董刚腾

住址（公共汽车站）：福建省龙岩市上杭县红学路 822 号腾院站（邮政编码：121747）。联系电话：75891116。电子邮箱：xyqkt@pnotblzi.transport.cn

Zhù zhǐ: Dǒng Gāng Téng Fújiàn Shěng Lóngyán Shì Shàng Háng Xiàn Hóng Xué Lù 822 Hào Téng Yuàn Zhàn (Yóuzhèng Biānmǎ: 121747). Liánxì Diànhuà: 75891116. Diànzǐ Yóuxiāng: xyqkt@pnotblzi.transport.cn

Gang Teng Dong, Teng Yuan Bus Station, 822 Hong Xue Road, Shanghang County, Longyan, Fujian. Postal Code: 121747. Phone Number: 75891116. E-mail: xyqkt@pnotblzi.transport.cn

642。姓名: 壤驷石刚

住址（公司）：福建省泉州市惠安县院轶路 942 号柱跃有限公司（邮政编码：691505）。联系电话：59009744。电子邮箱：cngfb@blzihjsk.biz.cn

Zhù zhǐ: Rǎngsì Shí Gāng Fújiàn Shěng Quánzhōu Shì Huìānxiàn Yuàn Yì Lù 942 Hào Zhù Yuè Yǒuxiàn Gōngsī (Yóuzhèng Biānmǎ: 691505). Liánxì Diànhuà: 59009744. Diànzǐ Yóuxiāng: cngfb@blzihjsk.biz.cn

Shi Gang Rangsi, Zhu Yue Corporation, 942 Yuan Yi Road, Huian County, Quanzhou, Fujian. Postal Code: 691505. Phone Number: 59009744. E-mail: cngfb@blzihjsk.biz.cn

643。姓名: 裴秀食

住址（酒店）：福建省平潭综合实验区平潭县克兆路 970 号乐寰酒店（邮政编码：606630）。联系电话：60723264。电子邮箱：nylse@czegapji.biz.cn

Zhù zhǐ: Péi Xiù Yì Fújiàn Shěng Píng Tán Zònghé Shíyàn Qū Píng Tán Xiàn Kè Zhào Lù 970 Hào Lè Huán Jiǔ Diàn (Yóuzhèng Biānmǎ: 606630). Liánxì Diànhuà: 60723264. Diànzǐ Yóuxiāng: nylse@czegapji.biz.cn

Xiu Yi Pei, Le Huan Hotel, 970 Ke Zhao Road, Pingtan County, Pingtan Comprehensive Experimental Area, Fujian. Postal Code: 606630. Phone Number: 60723264. E-mail: nylse@czegapji.biz.cn

644。姓名: 白际愈

住址（公园）：福建省南平市邵武市顺泽路 938 号龙熔公园（邮政编码：845732）。联系电话：16079135。电子邮箱：lwdnh@ovqpfxsz.parks.cn

Zhù zhǐ: Bái Jì Yù Fújiàn Shěng Nánpíng Shì Shàowǔ Shì Shùn Zé Lù 938 Hào Lóng Róng Gōng Yuán（Yóuzhèng Biānmǎ：845732）. Liánxì Diànhuà：16079135. Diànzǐ Yóuxiāng：lwdnh@ovqpfxsz.parks.cn

Ji Yu Bai, Long Rong Park, 938 Shun Ze Road, Shaowu, Nanping, Fujian. Postal Code: 845732. Phone Number：16079135. E-mail：lwdnh@ovqpfxsz.parks.cn

645。姓名: 蔡绅发

住址（医院）：福建省龙岩市新罗区茂自路 392 号易郁医院（邮政编码：720546）。联系电话：71609261。电子邮箱：pyqia@tfhagqwl.health.cn

Zhù zhǐ: Cài Shēn Fā Fújiàn Shěng Lóngyán Shì Xīn Luō Qū Mào Zì Lù 392 Hào Yì Yù Yī Yuàn（Yóuzhèng Biānmǎ：720546）. Liánxì Diànhuà：71609261. Diànzǐ Yóuxiāng：pyqia@tfhagqwl.health.cn

Shen Fa Cai, Yi Yu Hospital, 392 Mao Zi Road, Silla District, Longyan, Fujian. Postal Code: 720546. Phone Number：71609261. E-mail：pyqia@tfhagqwl.health.cn

646。姓名: 沈澜进

住址（大学）：福建省福州市闽清县九近大学涛己路 588 号（邮政编码：922921）。联系电话：41195200。电子邮箱：ogydu@ldhaqkrm.edu.cn

Zhù zhǐ: Shěn Lán Jìn Fújiàn Shěng Fúzhōu Shì Mǐn Qīng Xiàn Jiǔ Jìn DàxuéTāo Jǐ Lù 588 Hào（Yóuzhèng Biānmǎ：922921）. Liánxì Diànhuà：41195200. Diànzǐ Yóuxiāng：ogydu@ldhaqkrm.edu.cn

Lan Jin Shen, Jiu Jin University, 588 Tao Ji Road, Minqing County, Fuzhou, Fujian. Postal Code: 922921. Phone Number：41195200. E-mail：ogydu@ldhaqkrm.edu.cn

647。姓名: 郭屹宝

住址（家庭）：福建省泉州市泉港区石友路 159 号盛可公寓 33 层 481 室
（邮政编码：922703）。联系电话：77452615。电子邮箱：
ilmfx@ydaprwtl.cn

Zhù zhǐ: Guō Yì Bǎo Fújiàn Shěng Quánzhōu Shì Quán Gǎng Qū Shí Yǒu Lù 159 Hào
Shèng Kě Gōng Yù 33 Céng 481 Shì (Yóuzhèng Biānmǎ：922703). Liánxì Diànhuà：
77452615. Diànzǐ Yóuxiāng：ilmfx@ydaprwtl.cn

Yi Bao Guo, Room# 481, Floor# 33, Sheng Ke Apartment, 159 Shi You Road,
Quangang District, Quanzhou, Fujian. Postal Code: 922703. Phone Number：
77452615. E-mail：ilmfx@ydaprwtl.cn

648。姓名: 桓兆盛

住址（酒店）：福建省平潭综合实验区平潭县宝福路 871 号人圣酒店（邮政
编码：358662）。联系电话：56083241。电子邮箱：ckhgt@aobhvqpj.biz.cn

Zhù zhǐ: Huán Zhào Chéng Fújiàn Shěng Píng Tán Zònghé Shíyàn Qū Píng Tán Xiàn
Bǎo Fú Lù 871 Hào Rén Shèng Jiǔ Diàn (Yóuzhèng Biānmǎ：358662). Liánxì
Diànhuà：56083241. Diànzǐ Yóuxiāng：ckhgt@aobhvqpj.biz.cn

Zhao Cheng Huan, Ren Sheng Hotel, 871 Bao Fu Road, Pingtan County, Pingtan
Comprehensive Experimental Area, Fujian. Postal Code: 358662. Phone Number：
56083241. E-mail：ckhgt@aobhvqpj.biz.cn

649。姓名: 鄢铁食

住址（公园）：福建省泉州市安溪县石立路 418 号跃冕公园（邮政编码：
206926）。联系电话：63599732。电子邮箱：vpoyk@qjcnamsb.parks.cn

Zhù zhǐ: Yān Tiě Sì Fújiàn Shěng Quánzhōu Shì Ānxī Xiàn Shí Lì Lù 418 Hào Yuè
Miǎn Gōng Yuán (Yóuzhèng Biānmǎ：206926). Liánxì Diànhuà：63599732.
Diànzǐ Yóuxiāng：vpoyk@qjcnamsb.parks.cn

Tie Si Yan, Yue Mian Park, 418 Shi Li Road, Anxi County, Quanzhou, Fujian. Postal
Code: 206926. Phone Number：63599732. E-mail：vpoyk@qjcnamsb.parks.cn

650。姓名: 栾臻陶

住址（公司）：福建省福州市晋安区民兵路 275 号顺黎有限公司（邮政编码：422912）。联系电话：55241123。电子邮箱：aifrh@xpntirbz.biz.cn

Zhù zhǐ: Luán Zhēn Táo Fújiàn Shěng Fúzhōu Shì Jìn Ān Qū Mín Bīng Lù 275 Hào Shùn Lí Yǒuxiàn Gōngsī（Yóuzhèng Biānmǎ：422912). Liánxì Diànhuà：55241123. Diànzǐ Yóuxiāng：aifrh@xpntirbz.biz.cn

Zhen Tao Luan, Shun Li Corporation, 275 Min Bing Road, Jinan District, Fuzhou, Fujian. Postal Code: 422912. Phone Number：55241123. E-mail：aifrh@xpntirbz.biz.cn

651。姓名: 夏晖恩

住址（酒店）：福建省宁德市柘荣县宝亮路 226 号可跃酒店（邮政编码：445868）。联系电话：44752753。电子邮箱：luzxf@wpcmqtld.biz.cn

Zhù zhǐ: Xià Huī Ēn Fújiàn Shěng Níngdé Shì Zhè Róngxiàn Bǎo Liàng Lù 226 Hào Kě Yuè Jiǔ Diàn（Yóuzhèng Biānmǎ：445868). Liánxì Diànhuà：44752753. Diànzǐ Yóuxiāng：luzxf@wpcmqtld.biz.cn

Hui En Xia, Ke Yue Hotel, 226 Bao Liang Road, Zherong County, Ningde, Fujian. Postal Code: 445868. Phone Number：44752753. E-mail：luzxf@wpcmqtld.biz.cn

652。姓名: 唐计友

住址（大学）：福建省平潭综合实验区平潭县轼腾大学土俊路 927 号（邮政编码：918368）。联系电话：40319006。电子邮箱：lrzfa@cadyilwx.edu.cn

Zhù zhǐ: Táng Jì Yǒu Fújiàn Shěng Píng Tán Zònghé Shíyàn Qū Píng Tán Xiàn Shì Téng DàxuéTǔ Jùn Lù 927 Hào（Yóuzhèng Biānmǎ：918368). Liánxì Diànhuà：40319006. Diànzǐ Yóuxiāng：lrzfa@cadyilwx.edu.cn

Ji You Tang, Shi Teng University, 927 Tu Jun Road, Pingtan County, Pingtan Comprehensive Experimental Area, Fujian. Postal Code: 918368. Phone Number：40319006. E-mail：lrzfa@cadyilwx.edu.cn

653。姓名: 虞乐翼

住址（广场）：福建省平潭综合实验区平潭县懂际路 229 号鸣茂广场（邮政编码：643539）。联系电话：60175907。电子邮箱：vfgpm@lixmabor.squares.cn

Zhù zhǐ: Yú Lè Yì Fújiàn Shěng Píng Tán Zònghé Shíyàn Qū Píng Tán Xiàn Dǒng Jì Lù 229 Hào Míng Mào Guǎng Chǎng （Yóuzhèng Biānmǎ：643539). Liánxì Diànhuà: 60175907. Diànzǐ Yóuxiāng：vfgpm@lixmabor.squares.cn

Le Yi Yu, Ming Mao Square, 229 Dong Ji Road, Pingtan County, Pingtan Comprehensive Experimental Area, Fujian. Postal Code: 643539. Phone Number：60175907. E-mail：vfgpm@lixmabor.squares.cn

654。姓名: 仲原亮

住址（博物院）：福建省泉州市泉港区成楚路 661 号泉州博物馆（邮政编码：861701）。联系电话：51734194。电子邮箱：eqwfj@kfecauwy.museums.cn

Zhù zhǐ: Zhòng Yuán Liàng Fújiàn Shěng Quánzhōu Shì Quán Gǎng Qū Chéng Chǔ Lù 661 Hào Quánzōu Bó Wù Guǎn （Yóuzhèng Biānmǎ：861701). Liánxì Diànhuà: 51734194. Diànzǐ Yóuxiāng：eqwfj@kfecauwy.museums.cn

Yuan Liang Zhong, Quanzhou Museum, 661 Cheng Chu Road, Quangang District, Quanzhou, Fujian. Postal Code: 861701. Phone Number：51734194. E-mail：eqwfj@kfecauwy.museums.cn

655。姓名: 简轼鸣

住址（公园）：福建省莆田市荔城区屹世路 158 号龙食公园（邮政编码：143507）。联系电话：98424483。电子邮箱：lehkp@kbwyefxg.parks.cn

Zhù zhǐ: Jiǎn Shì Míng Fújiàn Shěng Pútián Shì Lì Chéngqū Yì Shì Lù 158 Hào Lóng Sì Gōng Yuán （Yóuzhèng Biānmǎ： 143507). Liánxì Diànhuà： 98424483. Diànzǐ Yóuxiāng： lehkp@kbwyefxg.parks.cn

Shi Ming Jian, Long Si Park, 158 Yi Shi Road, Licheng District, Putian, Fujian. Postal Code: 143507. Phone Number： 98424483. E-mail： lehkp@kbwyefxg.parks.cn

656。姓名：阎鸣迅

住址（广场）： 福建省莆田市涵江区强谢路 886 号郁焯广场 （邮政编码： 479632）。联系电话： 92000777。电子邮箱： lwkhs@qedfcoua.squares.cn

Zhù zhǐ: Yán Míng Xùn Fújiàn Shěng Pútián Shì Hánjiāng Qū Qiáng Xiè Lù 886 Hào Yù Zhuō Guǎng Chǎng （Yóuzhèng Biānmǎ： 479632). Liánxì Diànhuà： 92000777. Diànzǐ Yóuxiāng： lwkhs@qedfcoua.squares.cn

Ming Xun Yan, Yu Zhuo Square, 886 Qiang Xie Road, Hanjiang District, Putian, Fujian. Postal Code: 479632. Phone Number： 92000777. E-mail： lwkhs@qedfcoua.squares.cn

657。姓名：国淹茂

住址（酒店）： 福建省莆田市仙游县刚中路 289 号南禹酒店 （邮政编码： 666723）。联系电话： 50337246。电子邮箱： vnxyi@snthioyl.biz.cn

Zhù zhǐ: Guó Yān Mào Fújiàn Shěng Pútián Shì Xiān Yóu Xiàn Gāng Zhōng Lù 289 Hào Nán Yǔ Jiǔ Diàn （Yóuzhèng Biānmǎ： 666723). Liánxì Diànhuà： 50337246. Diànzǐ Yóuxiāng： vnxyi@snthioyl.biz.cn

Yan Mao Guo, Nan Yu Hotel, 289 Gang Zhong Road, Xianyou County, Putian, Fujian. Postal Code: 666723. Phone Number： 50337246. E-mail： vnxyi@snthioyl.biz.cn

658。姓名：萧南宽

住址（大学）：福建省漳州市长泰区守泽大学圣恩路 619 号（邮政编码：792008）。联系电话：44144598。电子邮箱：hxwlv@xpundgyl.edu.cn

Zhù zhǐ: Xiāo Nán Kuān Fújiàn Shěng Zhāngzhōu Shì Zhǎng Tài Qū Shǒu Zé DàxuéShèng Ēn Lù 619 Hào（Yóuzhèng Biānmǎ：792008). Liánxì Diànhuà：44144598. Diànzǐ Yóuxiāng：hxwlv@xpundgyl.edu.cn

Nan Kuan Xiao, Shou Ze University, 619 Sheng En Road, Changtai District, Zhangzhou, Fujian. Postal Code: 792008. Phone Number：44144598. E-mail：hxwlv@xpundgyl.edu.cn

659。姓名:萧食昌

住址（公司）：福建省漳州市龙文区成不路 104 号南腾有限公司（邮政编码：813777）。联系电话：93770975。电子邮箱：pvnia@bqmolfdw.biz.cn

Zhù zhǐ: Xiāo Yì Chāng Fújiàn Shěng Zhāngzhōu Shì Lóng Wén Qū Chéng Bù Lù 104 Hào Nán Téng Yǒuxiàn Gōngsī（Yóuzhèng Biānmǎ：813777). Liánxì Diànhuà：93770975. Diànzǐ Yóuxiāng：pvnia@bqmolfdw.biz.cn

Yi Chang Xiao, Nan Teng Corporation, 104 Cheng Bu Road, Longwen District, Zhangzhou, Fujian. Postal Code: 813777. Phone Number：93770975. E-mail：pvnia@bqmolfdw.biz.cn

660。姓名:杨宽红

住址（湖泊）：福建省泉州市石狮市钊科路 671 号洵强湖（邮政编码：319344）。联系电话：24916128。电子邮箱：upxfw@eylwodan.lakes.cn

Zhù zhǐ: Yáng Kuān Hóng Fújiàn Shěng Quánzhōu Shì Shíshī Shì Zhāo Kē Lù 671 Hào Xún Qiǎng Hú（Yóuzhèng Biānmǎ：319344). Liánxì Diànhuà：24916128. Diànzǐ Yóuxiāng：upxfw@eylwodan.lakes.cn

Kuan Hong Yang, Xun Qiang Lake, 671 Zhao Ke Road, Shishi, Quanzhou, Fujian. Postal Code: 319344. Phone Number：24916128. E-mail：upxfw@eylwodan.lakes.cn

CHAPTER 3: NAME, SURNAME & ADDRESSES (61-90)

661。姓名: 崔来陆

住址（公司）：福建省莆田市荔城区焯柱路 582 号嘉茂有限公司（邮政编码：484184）。联系电话：99485040。电子邮箱：xebhz@btwvfuie.biz.cn

Zhù zhǐ: Cuī Lái Lù Fújiàn Shěng Pútián Shì Lì Chéngqū Chāo Zhù Lù 582 Hào Jiā Mào Yǒuxiàn Gōngsī（Yóuzhèng Biānmǎ：484184). Liánxì Diànhuà：99485040. Diànzǐ Yóuxiāng：xebhz@btwvfuie.biz.cn

Lai Lu Cui, Jia Mao Corporation, 582 Chao Zhu Road, Licheng District, Putian, Fujian. Postal Code: 484184. Phone Number：99485040. E-mail：xebhz@btwvfuie.biz.cn

662。姓名: 师帆晗

住址（医院）：福建省福州市闽清县仓珏路 685 号刚浩医院（邮政编码：712583）。联系电话：79324416。电子邮箱：cabio@qurztxjn.health.cn

Zhù zhǐ: Shī Fān Hán Fújiàn Shěng Fúzhōu Shì Mǐn Qīng Xiàn Cāng Jué Lù 685 Hào Gāng Hào Yī Yuàn（Yóuzhèng Biānmǎ：712583). Liánxì Diànhuà：79324416. Diànzǐ Yóuxiāng：cabio@qurztxjn.health.cn

Fan Han Shi, Gang Hao Hospital, 685 Cang Jue Road, Minqing County, Fuzhou, Fujian. Postal Code: 712583. Phone Number：79324416. E-mail：cabio@qurztxjn.health.cn

663。姓名: 闵辙焯

住址（火车站）：福建省福州市闽侯县亭钢路 792 号福州站（邮政编码：907969）。联系电话：68623589。电子邮箱：tqwdo@gifcvhyz.chr.cn

Zhù zhǐ: Mǐn Zhé Zhuō Fújiàn Shěng Fúzhōu Shì Mǐn Hóu Xiàn Tíng Gāng Lù 792 Hào Fúzōu Zhàn（Yóuzhèng Biānmǎ：907969). Liánxì Diànhuà：68623589. Diànzǐ Yóuxiāng：tqwdo@gifcvhyz.chr.cn

Zhe Zhuo Min, Fuzhou Railway Station, 792 Ting Gang Road, Minhou County, Fuzhou, Fujian. Postal Code: 907969. Phone Number：68623589. E-mail：tqwdo@gifcvhyz.chr.cn

664。姓名: 戴恩甫

住址（火车站）：福建省莆田市仙游县克铁路 942 号莆田站（邮政编码：940770）。联系电话：82954752。电子邮箱：dybgu@jweyzdhp.chr.cn

Zhù zhǐ: Dài Ēn Fǔ Fújiàn Shěng Pútián Shì Xiān Yóu Xiàn Kè Fū Lù 942 Hào Pútián Zhàn （Yóuzhèng Biānmǎ：940770). Liánxì Diànhuà：82954752. Diànzǐ Yóuxiāng：dybgu@jweyzdhp.chr.cn

En Fu Dai, Putian Railway Station, 942 Ke Fu Road, Xianyou County, Putian, Fujian. Postal Code: 940770. Phone Number：82954752. E-mail：dybgu@jweyzdhp.chr.cn

665。姓名: 陶院化

住址（医院）：福建省厦门市翔安区王世路 507 号钦顺医院（邮政编码：439885）。联系电话：14919387。电子邮箱：hbczn@hvuaczsk.health.cn

Zhù zhǐ: Táo Yuàn Huā Fújiàn Shěng Xiàmén Shì Xiáng Ān Qū Wáng Shì Lù 507 Hào Qīn Shùn Yī Yuàn （Yóuzhèng Biānmǎ：439885). Liánxì Diànhuà：14919387. Diànzǐ Yóuxiāng：hbczn@hvuaczsk.health.cn

Yuan Hua Tao, Qin Shun Hospital, 507 Wang Shi Road, Xiangan District, Xiamen, Fujian. Postal Code: 439885. Phone Number：14919387. E-mail：hbczn@hvuaczsk.health.cn

666。姓名: 范龙立

住址（机场）：福建省三明市泰宁县秀化路 474 号三明臻智国际机场（邮政编码：233707）。联系电话：61308597。电子邮箱：egwra@egimjsfh.airports.cn

Zhù zhǐ: Fàn Lóng Lì Fújiàn Shěng Sānmíng Shì Tài Níngxiàn Xiù Huà Lù 474 Hào ānmíng Zhēn Zhì Guó Jì Jī Chǎng (Yóuzhèng Biānmǎ：233707). Liánxì Diànhuà：61308597. Diànzǐ Yóuxiāng：egwra@egimjsfh.airports.cn

Long Li Fan, Sanming Zhen Zhi International Airport, 474 Xiu Hua Road, Taining County, Sanming, Fujian. Postal Code: 233707. Phone Number：61308597. E-mail：egwra@egimjsfh.airports.cn

667。姓名: 宣启民

住址（大学）：福建省宁德市福鼎市鸣汉大学彬盛路 889 号（邮政编码：413483）。联系电话：81149878。电子邮箱：xicjm@frvyxgab.edu.cn

Zhù zhǐ: Xuān Qǐ Mín Fújiàn Shěng Níngdé Shì Fú Dǐng Shì Míng Hàn DàxuéBīn Shèng Lù 889 Hào (Yóuzhèng Biānmǎ：413483). Liánxì Diànhuà：81149878. Diànzǐ Yóuxiāng：xicjm@frvyxgab.edu.cn

Qi Min Xuan, Ming Han University, 889 Bin Sheng Road, Fuding City, Ningde, Fujian. Postal Code: 413483. Phone Number：81149878. E-mail：xicjm@frvyxgab.edu.cn

668。姓名: 琴仲德

住址（寺庙）：福建省平潭综合实验区平潭县焯人路 944 号腾白寺（邮政编码：795741）。联系电话：85577407。电子邮箱：dizxk@cxwezjgv.god.cn

Zhù zhǐ: Qín Zhòng Dé Fújiàn Shěng Píng Tán Zònghé Shíyàn Qū Píng Tán Xiàn Chāo Rén Lù 944 Hào Téng Bái Sì (Yóuzhèng Biānmǎ：795741). Liánxì Diànhuà：85577407. Diànzǐ Yóuxiāng：dizxk@cxwezjgv.god.cn

Zhong De Qin, Teng Bai Temple, 944 Chao Ren Road, Pingtan County, Pingtan Comprehensive Experimental Area, Fujian. Postal Code: 795741. Phone Number：85577407. E-mail：dizxk@cxwezjgv.god.cn

669。姓名: 汝轶译

住址（家庭）：福建省三明市明溪县茂光路 646 号福郁公寓 17 层 919 室
（邮政编码：704270）。联系电话：32475976。电子邮箱：
twyzf@xtrazpcs.cn

Zhù zhǐ: Rǔ Yì Yì Fújiàn Shěng Sānmíng Shì Míng Xī Xiàn Mào Guāng Lù 646 Hào Fú
Yù Gōng Yù 17 Céng 919 Shì (Yóuzhèng Biānmǎ：704270). Liánxì Diànhuà：
32475976. Diànzǐ Yóuxiāng：twyzf@xtrazpcs.cn

Yi Yi Ru, Room# 919, Floor# 17, Fu Yu Apartment, 646 Mao Guang Road, Mingxi
County, Sanming, Fujian. Postal Code: 704270. Phone Number：32475976. E-mail：
twyzf@xtrazpcs.cn

670。姓名: 熊自强

住址（火车站）：福建省漳州市漳浦县游臻路 569 号漳州站（邮政编码：
705750）。联系电话：79431361。电子邮箱：puwxy@ocxinmvw.chr.cn

Zhù zhǐ: Xióng Zì Qiáng Fújiàn Shěng Zhāngzhōu Shì Zhāng Pǔ Xiàn Yóu Zhēn Lù
569 Hào Zāngzōu Zhàn (Yóuzhèng Biānmǎ：705750). Liánxì Diànhuà：79431361.
Diànzǐ Yóuxiāng：puwxy@ocxinmvw.chr.cn

Zi Qiang Xiong, Zhangzhou Railway Station, 569 You Zhen Road, Zhangpu County,
Zhangzhou, Fujian. Postal Code: 705750. Phone Number：79431361. E-mail：
puwxy@ocxinmvw.chr.cn

671。姓名: 殳勇俊

住址（公司）：福建省三明市沙县区盛腾路 878 号先冠有限公司（邮政编码：
950791）。联系电话：34213428。电子邮箱：ivqrm@zqfwdhvt.biz.cn

Zhù zhǐ: Shū Yǒng Jùn Fújiàn Shěng Sānmíng Shì Shāxiàn Qū Shèng Téng Lù 878
Hào Xiān Guàn Yǒuxiàn Gōngsī (Yóuzhèng Biānmǎ：950791). Liánxì Diànhuà：
34213428. Diànzǐ Yóuxiāng：ivqrm@zqfwdhvt.biz.cn

Yong Jun Shu, Xian Guan Corporation, 878 Sheng Teng Road, Shaxian District, Sanming, Fujian. Postal Code: 950791. Phone Number：34213428. E-mail：ivqrm@zqfwdhvt.biz.cn

672。姓名: 孙金铭

住址（大学）：福建省平潭综合实验区平潭县克星大学秀石路 721 号（邮政编码：735503）。联系电话：55978097。电子邮箱：flcsh@pxjrtvli.edu.cn

Zhù zhǐ: Sūn Jīn Míng Fújiàn Shěng Píng Tán Zònghé Shíyàn Qū Píng Tán Xiàn Kè Xīng DàxuéXiù Dàn Lù 721 Hào (Yóuzhèng Biānmǎ：735503). Liánxì Diànhuà：55978097. Diànzǐ Yóuxiāng：flcsh@pxjrtvli.edu.cn

Jin Ming Sun, Ke Xing University, 721 Xiu Dan Road, Pingtan County, Pingtan Comprehensive Experimental Area, Fujian. Postal Code: 735503. Phone Number：55978097. E-mail：flcsh@pxjrtvli.edu.cn

673。姓名: 亢来仓

住址（酒店）：福建省漳州市龙文区可毅路 468 号译敬酒店（邮政编码：451755）。联系电话：38597752。电子邮箱：fytqi@dwgynomp.biz.cn

Zhù zhǐ: Kàng Lái Cāng Fújiàn Shěng Zhāngzhōu Shì Lóng Wén Qū Kě Yì Lù 468 Hào Yì Jìng Jiǔ Diàn (Yóuzhèng Biānmǎ：451755). Liánxì Diànhuà：38597752. Diànzǐ Yóuxiāng：fytqi@dwgynomp.biz.cn

Lai Cang Kang, Yi Jing Hotel, 468 Ke Yi Road, Longwen District, Zhangzhou, Fujian. Postal Code: 451755. Phone Number：38597752. E-mail：fytqi@dwgynomp.biz.cn

674。姓名: 晋隆员

住址（公共汽车站）：福建省泉州市泉港区发敬路 212 号龙钊站（邮政编码：866343）。联系电话：78698187。电子邮箱：ybrtn@qljyiwpr.transport.cn

Zhù zhǐ: Jìn Lóng Yún Fújiàn Shěng Quánzhōu Shì Quán Gǎng Qū Fā Jìng Lù 212 Hào Lóng Zhāo Zhàn (Yóuzhèng Biānmǎ: 866343). Liánxì Diànhuà: 78698187. Diànzǐ Yóuxiāng: ybrtn@qljyiwpr.transport.cn

Long Yun Jin, Long Zhao Bus Station, 212 Fa Jing Road, Quangang District, Quanzhou, Fujian. Postal Code: 866343. Phone Number: 78698187. E-mail: ybrtn@qljyiwpr.transport.cn

675。姓名: 鄂轼强

住址（寺庙）：福建省龙岩市漳平市居克路 784 号智豹寺（邮政编码：880993）。联系电话：93437755。电子邮箱：qkxhu@davuflcb.god.cn

Zhù zhǐ: È Shì Qiǎng Fújiàn Shěng Lóngyán Shì Zhāng Píngshì Jū Kè Lù 784 Hào Zhì Bào Sì (Yóuzhèng Biānmǎ: 880993). Liánxì Diànhuà: 93437755. Diànzǐ Yóuxiāng: qkxhu@davuflcb.god.cn

Shi Qiang E, Zhi Bao Temple, 784 Ju Ke Road, Zhangping, Longyan, Fujian. Postal Code: 880993. Phone Number: 93437755. E-mail: qkxhu@davuflcb.god.cn

676。姓名: 殷茂辙

住址（广场）：福建省福州市连江县维辉路 396 号食绅广场（邮政编码：410245）。联系电话：92571642。电子邮箱：klasp@rfyusgml.squares.cn

Zhù zhǐ: Yīn Mào Zhé Fújiàn Shěng Fúzhōu Shì Lián Jiāng Xiàn Wéi Huī Lù 396 Hào Yì Shēn Guǎng Chǎng (Yóuzhèng Biānmǎ: 410245). Liánxì Diànhuà: 92571642. Diànzǐ Yóuxiāng: klasp@rfyusgml.squares.cn

Mao Zhe Yin, Yi Shen Square, 396 Wei Hui Road, Lianjiang County, Fuzhou, Fujian. Postal Code: 410245. Phone Number: 92571642. E-mail: klasp@rfyusgml.squares.cn

677。姓名: 盖翼汉

住址（广场）：福建省福州市马尾区大楚路 412 号轼山广场（邮政编码：873497）。联系电话：35843773。电子邮箱：zefxu@mbwnpglo.squares.cn

Zhù zhǐ: Gài Yì Hàn Fújiàn Shěng Fúzhōu Shì Mǎwěi Qū Dài Chǔ Lù 412 Hào Shì Shān Guǎng Chǎng（Yóuzhèng Biānmǎ：873497）. Liánxì Diànhuà：35843773. Diànzǐ Yóuxiāng：zefxu@mbwnpglo.squares.cn

Yi Han Gai, Shi Shan Square, 412 Dai Chu Road, Mawei District, Fuzhou, Fujian. Postal Code: 873497. Phone Number：35843773. E-mail：zefxu@mbwnpglo.squares.cn

678。姓名: 钱坤领

住址（医院）：福建省南平市邵武市计鹤路 918 号澜九医院（邮政编码：484156）。联系电话：45987726。电子邮箱：vzenl@snmiewdg.health.cn

Zhù zhǐ: Qián Kūn Lǐng Fújiàn Shěng Nánpíng Shì Shàowǔ Shì Jì Hè Lù 918 Hào Lán Jiǔ Yī Yuàn（Yóuzhèng Biānmǎ：484156）. Liánxì Diànhuà：45987726. Diànzǐ Yóuxiāng：vzenl@snmiewdg.health.cn

Kun Ling Qian, Lan Jiu Hospital, 918 Ji He Road, Shaowu, Nanping, Fujian. Postal Code: 484156. Phone Number：45987726. E-mail：vzenl@snmiewdg.health.cn

679。姓名: 钮中金

住址（家庭）：福建省漳州市长泰区焯圣路 442 号辉易公寓 49 层 654 室（邮政编码：913982）。联系电话：23988343。电子邮箱：emryq@vmjlipwg.cn

Zhù zhǐ: Niǔ Zhōng Jīn Fújiàn Shěng Zhāngzhōu Shì Zhǎng Tài Qū Zhuō Shèng Lù 442 Hào Huī Yì Gōng Yù 49 Céng 654 Shì（Yóuzhèng Biānmǎ：913982）. Liánxì Diànhuà：23988343. Diànzǐ Yóuxiāng：emryq@vmjlipwg.cn

Zhong Jin Niu, Room# 654, Floor# 49, Hui Yi Apartment, 442 Zhuo Sheng Road, Changtai District, Zhangzhou, Fujian. Postal Code: 913982. Phone Number：23988343. E-mail：emryq@vmjlipwg.cn

680。姓名：计宝化

住址（寺庙）：福建省南平市建瓯市九化路 347 号中焯寺（邮政编码：138077）。联系电话：68041884。电子邮箱：hqzbk@qejfhlkb.god.cn

Zhù zhǐ: Jì Bǎo Huā Fújiàn Shěng Nánpíng Shì Jiàn Ōu Shì Jiǔ Huā Lù 347 Hào Zhōng Zhuō Sì (Yóuzhèng Biānmǎ：138077). Liánxì Diànhuà：68041884. Diànzǐ Yóuxiāng：hqzbk@qejfhlkb.god.cn

Bao Hua Ji, Zhong Zhuo Temple, 347 Jiu Hua Road, Jianou City, Nanping, Fujian. Postal Code: 138077. Phone Number：68041884. E-mail：hqzbk@qejfhlkb.god.cn

681。姓名：詹冠浩

住址（家庭）：福建省莆田市城厢区振伦路 414 号九铁公寓 1 层 336 室（邮政编码：751881）。联系电话：86261394。电子邮箱：opsln@tjoipeyc.cn

Zhù zhǐ: Zhān Guàn Hào Fújiàn Shěng Pútián Shì Chéngxiāng Qū Zhèn Lún Lù 414 Hào Jiǔ Fū Gōng Yù 1 Céng 336 Shì (Yóuzhèng Biānmǎ：751881). Liánxì Diànhuà：86261394. Diànzǐ Yóuxiāng：opsln@tjoipeyc.cn

Guan Hao Zhan, Room# 336, Floor# 1, Jiu Fu Apartment, 414 Zhen Lun Road, Chengxiang District, Putian, Fujian. Postal Code: 751881. Phone Number：86261394. E-mail：opsln@tjoipeyc.cn

682。姓名：弘黎克

住址（大学）：福建省平潭综合实验区平潭县成庆大学成翼路 111 号（邮政编码：343972）。联系电话：64700054。电子邮箱：rcgsj@tfbnaijv.edu.cn

Zhù zhǐ: Hóng Lí Kè Fújiàn Shěng Píng Tán Zònghé Shíyàn Qū Píng Tán Xiàn Chéng Qìng DàxuéChéng Yì Lù 111 Hào (Yóuzhèng Biānmǎ：343972). Liánxì Diànhuà：64700054. Diànzǐ Yóuxiāng：rcgsj@tfbnaijv.edu.cn

Li Ke Hong, Cheng Qing University, 111 Cheng Yi Road, Pingtan County, Pingtan Comprehensive Experimental Area, Fujian. Postal Code: 343972. Phone Number：64700054. E-mail：rcgsj@tfbnaijv.edu.cn

683。姓名: 闫坤彬

住址（广场）：福建省泉州市金门县圣歧路 419 号俊水广场（邮政编码：259026）。联系电话：86508742。电子邮箱：qjzft@ywezxkjs.squares.cn

Zhù zhǐ: Yán Kūn Bīn Fújiàn Shěng Quánzhōu Shì Jīnmén Xiàn Shèng Qí Lù 419 Hào Jùn Shuǐ Guǎng Chǎng（Yóuzhèng Biānmǎ：259026). Liánxì Diànhuà：86508742. Diànzǐ Yóuxiāng：qjzft@ywezxkjs.squares.cn

Kun Bin Yan, Jun Shui Square, 419 Sheng Qi Road, Kinmen County, Quanzhou, Fujian. Postal Code: 259026. Phone Number：86508742. E-mail：qjzft@ywezxkjs.squares.cn

684。姓名: 雷振涛

住址（公园）：福建省龙岩市新罗区国继路 733 号盛国公园（邮政编码：407798）。联系电话：71623960。电子邮箱：pghdl@lbqtpsyr.parks.cn

Zhù zhǐ: Léi Zhèn Tāo Fújiàn Shěng Lóngyán Shì Xīn Luō Qū Guó Jì Lù 733 Hào Chéng Guó Gōng Yuán（Yóuzhèng Biānmǎ：407798). Liánxì Diànhuà：71623960. Diànzǐ Yóuxiāng：pghdl@lbqtpsyr.parks.cn

Zhen Tao Lei, Cheng Guo Park, 733 Guo Ji Road, Silla District, Longyan, Fujian. Postal Code: 407798. Phone Number：71623960. E-mail：pghdl@lbqtpsyr.parks.cn

685。姓名: 富隆居

住址（公共汽车站）：福建省泉州市安溪县南人路 353 号山星站（邮政编码：690309）。联系电话：96567801。电子邮箱：xvnpo@tyzksmjr.transport.cn

Zhù zhǐ: Fù Lóng Jū Fújiàn Shěng Quánzhōu Shì Ānxī Xiàn Nán Rén Lù 353 Hào Shān Xīng Zhàn (Yóuzhèng Biānmǎ：690309). Liánxì Diànhuà：96567801. Diànzǐ Yóuxiāng：xvnpo@tyzksmjr.transport.cn

Long Ju Fu, Shan Xing Bus Station, 353 Nan Ren Road, Anxi County, Quanzhou, Fujian. Postal Code: 690309. Phone Number：96567801. E-mail：xvnpo@tyzksmjr.transport.cn

686。姓名: 计刚星

住址（家庭）：福建省泉州市惠安县员白路 122 号风甫公寓 35 层 434 室（邮政编码：930760）。联系电话：11115024。电子邮箱：nfqhr@gxkfervo.cn

Zhù zhǐ: Jì Gāng Xīng Fújiàn Shěng Quánzhōu Shì Huìānxiàn Yuán Bái Lù 122 Hào Fēng Fǔ Gōng Yù 35 Céng 434 Shì (Yóuzhèng Biānmǎ：930760). Liánxì Diànhuà：11115024. Diànzǐ Yóuxiāng：nfqhr@gxkfervo.cn

Gang Xing Ji, Room# 434, Floor# 35, Feng Fu Apartment, 122 Yuan Bai Road, Huian County, Quanzhou, Fujian. Postal Code: 930760. Phone Number：11115024. E-mail：nfqhr@gxkfervo.cn

687。姓名: 庾亭翼

住址（机场）：福建省漳州市龙海区尚智路 331 号漳州全焯国际机场（邮政编码：952305）。联系电话：83220972。电子邮箱：sntgh@wkzmuaqr.airports.cn

Zhù zhǐ: Yǔ Tíng Yì Fújiàn Shěng Zhāngzhōu Shì Lóng Hǎiqū Shàng Zhì Lù 331 Hào Zāngzōu Quán Zhuō Guó Jì Jī Chǎng (Yóuzhèng Biānmǎ：952305). Liánxì Diànhuà：83220972. Diànzǐ Yóuxiāng：sntgh@wkzmuaqr.airports.cn

Ting Yi Yu, Zhangzhou Quan Zhuo International Airport, 331 Shang Zhi Road, Longhai District, Zhangzhou, Fujian. Postal Code: 952305. Phone Number：83220972. E-mail：sntgh@wkzmuaqr.airports.cn

688。姓名: 蓝秀汉

住址（广场）：福建省厦门市同安区宽仲路 832 号阳食广场（邮政编码：126334）。联系电话：21571972。电子邮箱：ajrzt@gaswbmyj.squares.cn

Zhù zhǐ: Lán Xiù Hàn Fújiàn Shěng Xiàmén Shì Tóngān Qū Kuān Zhòng Lù 832 Hào Yáng Shí Guǎng Chǎng（Yóuzhèng Biānmǎ：126334). Liánxì Diànhuà：21571972. Diànzǐ Yóuxiāng：ajrzt@gaswbmyj.squares.cn

Xiu Han Lan, Yang Shi Square, 832 Kuan Zhong Road, Tongan District, Xiamen, Fujian. Postal Code: 126334. Phone Number：21571972. E-mail：ajrzt@gaswbmyj.squares.cn

689。姓名: 莘斌食

住址（寺庙）：福建省龙岩市新罗区轶甫路 491 号石水寺（邮政编码：921853）。联系电话：83062002。电子邮箱：bgdue@tmjyqxbg.god.cn

Zhù zhǐ: Shēn Bīn Shí Fújiàn Shěng Lóngyán Shì Xīn Luō Qū Yì Fǔ Lù 491 Hào Shí Shuǐ Sì（Yóuzhèng Biānmǎ：921853). Liánxì Diànhuà：83062002. Diànzǐ Yóuxiāng：bgdue@tmjyqxbg.god.cn

Bin Shi Shen, Shi Shui Temple, 491 Yi Fu Road, Silla District, Longyan, Fujian. Postal Code: 921853. Phone Number：83062002. E-mail：bgdue@tmjyqxbg.god.cn

690。姓名: 乐盛己

住址（酒店）：福建省三明市沙县区仲坚路 700 号源敬酒店（邮政编码：814793）。联系电话：17008367。电子邮箱：dxhlg@uqrjeald.biz.cn

Zhù zhǐ: Yuè Chéng Jǐ Fújiàn Shěng Sānmíng Shì Shāxiàn Qū Zhòng Jiān Lù 700 Hào Yuán Jìng Jiǔ Diàn（Yóuzhèng Biānmǎ：814793). Liánxì Diànhuà：17008367. Diànzǐ Yóuxiāng：dxhlg@uqrjeald.biz.cn

Cheng Ji Yue, Yuan Jing Hotel, 700 Zhong Jian Road, Shaxian District, Sanming, Fujian. Postal Code: 814793. Phone Number：17008367. E-mail：dxhlg@uqrjeald.biz.cn

CHAPTER 4: NAME, SURNAME & ADDRESSES (91-120)

691。姓名: 缑庆金

住址（公园）： 福建省莆田市荔城区译可路 683 号居征公园（邮政编码：626931）。联系电话：75641678。电子邮箱：watfd@ewtxhmik.parks.cn

Zhù zhǐ: Gōu Qìng Jīn Fújiàn Shěng Pútián Shì Lì Chéngqū Yì Kě Lù 683 Hào Jū Zhēng Gōng Yuán（Yóuzhèng Biānmǎ：626931）. Liánxì Diànhuà：75641678. Diànzǐ Yóuxiāng：watfd@ewtxhmik.parks.cn

Qing Jin Gou, Ju Zheng Park, 683 Yi Ke Road, Licheng District, Putian, Fujian. Postal Code: 626931. Phone Number：75641678. E-mail：watfd@ewtxhmik.parks.cn

692。姓名: 全澜科

住址（公司）： 福建省南平市光泽县舟汉路 160 号钢威有限公司（邮政编码：639305）。联系电话：20952693。电子邮箱：njfrp@nregsxmp.biz.cn

Zhù zhǐ: Quán Lán Kē Fújiàn Shěng Nánpíng Shì Guāngzé Xiàn Zhōu Hàn Lù 160 Hào Gāng Wēi Yǒuxiàn Gōngsī（Yóuzhèng Biānmǎ：639305）. Liánxì Diànhuà：20952693. Diànzǐ Yóuxiāng：njfrp@nregsxmp.biz.cn

Lan Ke Quan, Gang Wei Corporation, 160 Zhou Han Road, Guangze County, Nanping, Fujian. Postal Code: 639305. Phone Number：20952693. E-mail：njfrp@nregsxmp.biz.cn

693。姓名: 亢黎坡

住址（湖泊）： 福建省泉州市丰泽区译钢路 545 号屹坚湖（邮政编码：708180）。联系电话：50547367。电子邮箱：pnadt@hcextygb.lakes.cn

Zhù zhǐ: Kàng Lí Pō Fújiàn Shěng Quánzhōu Shì Fēng Zé Qū Yì Gāng Lù 545 Hào Yì Jiān Hú（Yóuzhèng Biānmǎ：708180）. Liánxì Diànhuà：50547367. Diànzǐ Yóuxiāng：pnadt@hcextygb.lakes.cn

Li Po Kang, Yi Jian Lake, 545 Yi Gang Road, Fengze District, Quanzhou, Fujian. Postal Code: 708180. Phone Number：50547367. E-mail：pnadt@hcextygb.lakes.cn

694。姓名: 邴陶乙

住址（火车站）：福建省三明市永安市学亮路 732 号三明站（邮政编码：782710）。联系电话：44300972。电子邮箱：qwdcu@gmqdycrx.chr.cn

Zhù zhǐ: Bǐng Táo Yǐ Fújiàn Shěng Sānmíng Shì Yǒngān Shì Xué Liàng Lù 732 Hào ānmíng Zhàn（Yóuzhèng Biānmǎ：782710). Liánxì Diànhuà：44300972. Diànzǐ Yóuxiāng：qwdcu@gmqdycrx.chr.cn

Tao Yi Bing, Sanming Railway Station, 732 Xue Liang Road, Yongan City, Sanming, Fujian. Postal Code: 782710. Phone Number：44300972. E-mail：qwdcu@gmqdycrx.chr.cn

695。姓名: 仇督葆焯

住址（大学）：福建省宁德市蕉城区院陆大学辙歧路 499 号（邮政编码：852848）。联系电话：50990588。电子邮箱：uqxpb@utocnski.edu.cn

Zhù zhǐ: Zhǎngdū Bǎo Chāo Fújiàn Shěng Níngdé Shì Jiāo Chéngqū Yuàn Liù DàxuéZhé Qí Lù 499 Hào（Yóuzhèng Biānmǎ：852848). Liánxì Diànhuà：50990588. Diànzǐ Yóuxiāng：uqxpb@utocnski.edu.cn

Bao Chao Zhangdu, Yuan Liu University, 499 Zhe Qi Road, Jiaocheng District, Ningde, Fujian. Postal Code: 852848. Phone Number：50990588. E-mail：uqxpb@utocnski.edu.cn

696。姓名: 宫澜圣

住址（酒店）：福建省龙岩市连城县珂舟路 395 号葆来酒店（邮政编码：857605）。联系电话：41701845。电子邮箱：uobcn@mjwutplq.biz.cn

Zhù zhǐ: Gōng Lán Shèng Fújiàn Shěng Lóngyán Shì Liánchéng Xiàn Kē Zhōu Lù 395 Hào Bǎo Lái Jiǔ Diàn (Yóuzhèng Biānmǎ: 857605). Liánxì Diànhuà: 41701845. Diànzǐ Yóuxiāng: uobcn@mjwutplq.biz.cn

Lan Sheng Gong, Bao Lai Hotel, 395 Ke Zhou Road, Liancheng County, Longyan, Fujian. Postal Code: 857605. Phone Number: 41701845. E-mail: uobcn@mjwutplq.biz.cn

697。姓名: 笪德独

住址（公园）：福建省泉州市石狮市食葆路 437 号淹熔公园（邮政编码：383599）。联系电话：30417981。电子邮箱：yihar@wfhpqeay.parks.cn

Zhù zhǐ: Dá Dé Dú Fújiàn Shěng Quánzhōu Shì Shíshī Shì Shí Bǎo Lù 437 Hào Yān Róng Gōng Yuán (Yóuzhèng Biānmǎ: 383599). Liánxì Diànhuà: 30417981. Diànzǐ Yóuxiāng: yihar@wfhpqeay.parks.cn

De Du Da, Yan Rong Park, 437 Shi Bao Road, Shishi, Quanzhou, Fujian. Postal Code: 383599. Phone Number: 30417981. E-mail: yihar@wfhpqeay.parks.cn

698。姓名: 鲜于晖胜

住址（寺庙）：福建省三明市将乐县坚坚路 798 号人翼寺（邮政编码：797710）。联系电话：24631761。电子邮箱：vkczm@zoxslaeh.god.cn

Zhù zhǐ: Xiānyú Huī Shēng Fújiàn Shěng Sānmíng Shì Jiāng Lè Xiàn Jiān Jiān Lù 798 Hào Rén Yì Sì (Yóuzhèng Biānmǎ: 797710). Liánxì Diànhuà: 24631761. Diànzǐ Yóuxiāng: vkczm@zoxslaeh.god.cn

Hui Sheng Xianyu, Ren Yi Temple, 798 Jian Jian Road, Jiangle County, Sanming, Fujian. Postal Code: 797710. Phone Number: 24631761. E-mail: vkczm@zoxslaeh.god.cn

699。姓名: 上官翰亚

住址（火车站）：福建省三明市明溪县近可路 938 号三明站（邮政编码：153009）。联系电话：35418967。电子邮箱：zskwv@gfupinmd.chr.cn

Zhù zhǐ: Shàngguān Hàn Yà Fújiàn Shěng Sānmíng Shì Míng Xī Xiàn Jìn Kě Lù 938 Hào ānmíng Zhàn (Yóuzhèng Biānmǎ: 153009). Liánxì Diànhuà: 35418967. Diànzǐ Yóuxiāng: zskwv@gfupinmd.chr.cn

Han Ya Shangguan, Sanming Railway Station, 938 Jin Ke Road, Mingxi County, Sanming, Fujian. Postal Code: 153009. Phone Number: 35418967. E-mail: zskwv@gfupinmd.chr.cn

700。姓名: 简昌沛

住址（公园）：福建省南平市延平区臻王路 894 号腾圣公园（邮政编码：909523）。联系电话：75740711。电子邮箱：mzndb@cqgsvtpd.parks.cn

Zhù zhǐ: Jiǎn Chāng Pèi Fújiàn Shěng Nánpíng Shì Yánpíng Qū Zhēn Wàng Lù 894 Hào Téng Shèng Gōng Yuán (Yóuzhèng Biānmǎ: 909523). Liánxì Diànhuà: 75740711. Diànzǐ Yóuxiāng: mzndb@cqgsvtpd.parks.cn

Chang Pei Jian, Teng Sheng Park, 894 Zhen Wang Road, Yanping District, Nanping, Fujian. Postal Code: 909523. Phone Number: 75740711. E-mail: mzndb@cqgsvtpd.parks.cn

701。姓名: 濮阳翼胜

住址（家庭）：福建省福州市仓山区锡亭路 101 号近大公寓 1 层 124 室（邮政编码：897097）。联系电话：82705793。电子邮箱：lubew@qmvfwtoe.cn

Zhù zhǐ: Púyáng Yì Shēng Fújiàn Shěng Fúzhōu Shì Cāng Shānqū Xī Tíng Lù 101 Hào Jìn Dài Gōng Yù 1 Céng 124 Shì (Yóuzhèng Biānmǎ: 897097). Liánxì Diànhuà: 82705793. Diànzǐ Yóuxiāng: lubew@qmvfwtoe.cn

Yi Sheng Puyang, Room# 124, Floor# 1, Jin Dai Apartment, 101 Xi Ting Road, Cangshan District, Fuzhou, Fujian. Postal Code: 897097. Phone Number: 82705793. E-mail: lubew@qmvfwtoe.cn

702。姓名: 颜尚水

住址（家庭）： 福建省福州市福清市奎晖路 497 号大全公寓 12 层 674 室
（邮政编码：330577）。联系电话：59349521。电子邮箱：
jdtia@lqkhsydw.cn

Zhù zhǐ: Yán Shàng Shuǐ Fújiàn Shěng Fúzhōu Shì Fúqīng Shì Kuí Huī Lù 497 Hào Dài
Quán Gōng Yù 12 Céng 674 Shì (Yóuzhèng Biānmǎ： 330577). Liánxì Diànhuà：
59349521. Diànzǐ Yóuxiāng： jdtia@lqkhsydw.cn

Shang Shui Yan, Room# 674, Floor# 12, Dai Quan Apartment, 497 Kui Hui Road,
Fuqing City, Fuzhou, Fujian. Postal Code: 330577. Phone Number： 59349521. E-
mail： jdtia@lqkhsydw.cn

703。姓名: 商食队

住址（湖泊）： 福建省福州市闽侯县屹人路 295 号宽懂湖（邮政编码：
572498）。联系电话：41729297。电子邮箱：wamsg@egiszxrw.lakes.cn

Zhù zhǐ: Shāng Sì Duì Fújiàn Shěng Fúzhōu Shì Mǐn Hóu Xiàn Yì Rén Lù 295 Hào
Kuān Dǒng Hú (Yóuzhèng Biānmǎ： 572498). Liánxì Diànhuà： 41729297. Diànzǐ
Yóuxiāng： wamsg@egiszxrw.lakes.cn

Si Dui Shang, Kuan Dong Lake, 295 Yi Ren Road, Minhou County, Fuzhou, Fujian.
Postal Code: 572498. Phone Number： 41729297. E-mail：
wamsg@egiszxrw.lakes.cn

704。姓名: 呼延盛隆

住址（公园）： 福建省厦门市思明区食轶路 576 号稼恩公园（邮政编码：
861601）。联系电话：50718538。电子邮箱：hgznu@qcztluph.parks.cn

Zhù zhǐ: Hūyán Shèng Lóng Fújiàn Shěng Xiàmén Shì Sī Míng Qū Shí Yì Lù 576 Hào
Jià Ēn Gōng Yuán (Yóuzhèng Biānmǎ： 861601). Liánxì Diànhuà： 50718538.
Diànzǐ Yóuxiāng： hgznu@qcztluph.parks.cn

Sheng Long Huyan, Jia En Park, 576 Shi Yi Road, Siming District, Xiamen, Fujian. Postal Code: 861601. Phone Number：50718538. E-mail：hgznu@qcztluph.parks.cn

705。姓名: 宿国柱

住址（公园）：福建省厦门市思明区近自路 575 号员石公园（邮政编码：283287）。联系电话：95021756。电子邮箱：ulktj@ohbgraxt.parks.cn

Zhù zhǐ: Sù Guó Zhù Fújiàn Shěng Xiàmén Shì Sī Míng Qū Jìn Zì Lù 575 Hào Yún Shí Gōng Yuán (Yóuzhèng Biānmǎ：283287). Liánxì Diànhuà：95021756. Diànzǐ Yóuxiāng：ulktj@ohbgraxt.parks.cn

Guo Zhu Su, Yun Shi Park, 575 Jin Zi Road, Siming District, Xiamen, Fujian. Postal Code: 283287. Phone Number：95021756. E-mail：ulktj@ohbgraxt.parks.cn

706。姓名: 盛渊熔

住址（家庭）：福建省泉州市南安市兆乐路 279 号舟南公寓 6 层 956 室（邮政编码：571098）。联系电话：86910474。电子邮箱：pgxqv@uavedfxp.cn

Zhù zhǐ: Shèng Yuān Róng Fújiàn Shěng Quánzhōu Shì Nánān Shì Zhào Lè Lù 279 Hào Zhōu Nán Gōng Yù 6 Céng 956 Shì (Yóuzhèng Biānmǎ：571098). Liánxì Diànhuà：86910474. Diànzǐ Yóuxiāng：pgxqv@uavedfxp.cn

Yuan Rong Sheng, Room# 956, Floor# 6, Zhou Nan Apartment, 279 Zhao Le Road, Nanan City, Quanzhou, Fujian. Postal Code: 571098. Phone Number：86910474. E-mail：pgxqv@uavedfxp.cn

707。姓名: 戴食宽

住址（家庭）：福建省莆田市仙游县中星路 426 号歧冕公寓 30 层 829 室（邮政编码：477378）。联系电话：82318723。电子邮箱：vbicj@hfvorqlx.cn

Zhù zhǐ: Dài Yì Kuān Fújiàn Shěng Pútián Shì Xiān Yóu Xiàn Zhòng Xīng Lù 426 Hào Qí Miǎn Gōng Yù 30 Céng 829 Shì (Yóuzhèng Biānmǎ：477378). Liánxì Diànhuà：82318723. Diànzǐ Yóuxiāng：vbicj@hfvorqlx.cn

Yi Kuan Dai, Room# 829, Floor# 30, Qi Mian Apartment, 426 Zhong Xing Road, Xianyou County, Putian, Fujian. Postal Code: 477378. Phone Number：82318723. E-mail：vbicj@hfvorqlx.cn

708。姓名: 蒙葛昌

住址（公园）：福建省漳州市云霄县院澜路 422 号盛胜公园（邮政编码：728572）。联系电话：54525543。电子邮箱：vnjam@adbjiwzg.parks.cn

Zhù zhǐ: Méng Gé Chāng Fújiàn Shěng Zhāngzhōu Shì Yúnxiāo Xiàn Yuàn Lán Lù 422 Hào Shèng Shēng Gōng Yuán (Yóuzhèng Biānmǎ：728572). Liánxì Diànhuà：54525543. Diànzǐ Yóuxiāng：vnjam@adbjiwzg.parks.cn

Ge Chang Meng, Sheng Sheng Park, 422 Yuan Lan Road, Yunxiao County, Zhangzhou, Fujian. Postal Code: 728572. Phone Number：54525543. E-mail：vnjam@adbjiwzg.parks.cn

709。姓名: 言跃豹

住址（公共汽车站）：福建省南平市顺昌县坚惟路 199 号原继站（邮政编码：648724）。联系电话：28799909。电子邮箱：isprg@lgxwjmak.transport.cn

Zhù zhǐ: Yán Yuè Bào Fújiàn Shěng Nánpíng Shì Shùn Chāng Xiàn Jiān Wéi Lù 199 Hào Yuán Jì Zhàn (Yóuzhèng Biānmǎ：648724). Liánxì Diànhuà：28799909. Diànzǐ Yóuxiāng：isprg@lgxwjmak.transport.cn

Yue Bao Yan, Yuan Ji Bus Station, 199 Jian Wei Road, Shunchang County, Nanping, Fujian. Postal Code: 648724. Phone Number：28799909. E-mail：isprg@lgxwjmak.transport.cn

710。姓名: 牧易俊

住址（医院）：福建省南平市邵武市铁全路 776 号勇独医院（邮政编码：194458）。联系电话：68939650。电子邮箱：jxdtk@vyjotisf.health.cn

Zhù zhǐ: Mù Yì Jùn Fújiàn Shěng Nánpíng Shì Shàowǔ Shì Tiě Quán Lù 776 Hào Yǒng Dú Yī Yuàn（Yóuzhèng Biānmǎ：194458). Liánxì Diànhuà：68939650. Diànzǐ Yóuxiāng：jxdtk@vyjotisf.health.cn

Yi Jun Mu, Yong Du Hospital, 776 Tie Quan Road, Shaowu, Nanping, Fujian. Postal Code: 194458. Phone Number：68939650. E-mail：jxdtk@vyjotisf.health.cn

711。姓名: 乜刚继

住址（酒店）：福建省莆田市涵江区翰昌路 994 号晗桥酒店（邮政编码：157613）。联系电话：83486374。电子邮箱：bfqyr@dukgsqct.biz.cn

Zhù zhǐ: Niè Gāng Jì Fújiàn Shěng Pútián Shì Hánjiāng Qū Hàn Chāng Lù 994 Hào Hán Qiáo Jiǔ Diàn（Yóuzhèng Biānmǎ：157613). Liánxì Diànhuà：83486374. Diànzǐ Yóuxiāng：bfqyr@dukgsqct.biz.cn

Gang Ji Nie, Han Qiao Hotel, 994 Han Chang Road, Hanjiang District, Putian, Fujian. Postal Code: 157613. Phone Number：83486374. E-mail：bfqyr@dukgsqct.biz.cn

712。姓名: 昌智黎

住址（博物院）：福建省南平市政和县熔己路 483 号南平博物馆（邮政编码：382584）。联系电话：73601280。电子邮箱：dcvpw@ajegrzlb.museums.cn

Zhù zhǐ: Chāng Zhì Lí Fújiàn Shěng Nánpíng Shì Zhènghé Xiàn Róng Jǐ Lù 483 Hào Nánpíng Bó Wù Guǎn（Yóuzhèng Biānmǎ：382584). Liánxì Diànhuà：73601280. Diànzǐ Yóuxiāng：dcvpw@ajegrzlb.museums.cn

Zhi Li Chang, Nanping Museum, 483 Rong Ji Road, Zhenghe County, Nanping, Fujian. Postal Code: 382584. Phone Number：73601280. E-mail：dcvpw@ajegrzlb.museums.cn

713。姓名: 宿世译

住址（公园）：福建省南平市顺昌县葛南路 303 号磊舟公园（邮政编码：774340）。联系电话：44002833。电子邮箱：qnzmd@pclbyuvh.parks.cn

Zhù zhǐ: Sù Shì Yì Fújiàn Shěng Nánpíng Shì Shùn Chāng Xiàn Gé Nán Lù 303 Hào Lěi Zhōu Gōng Yuán (Yóuzhèng Biānmǎ：774340). Liánxì Diànhuà：44002833. Diànzǐ Yóuxiāng：qnzmd@pclbyuvh.parks.cn

Shi Yi Su, Lei Zhou Park, 303 Ge Nan Road, Shunchang County, Nanping, Fujian. Postal Code: 774340. Phone Number：44002833. E-mail：qnzmd@pclbyuvh.parks.cn

714。姓名: 宁居锤

住址（博物院）：福建省福州市长乐区磊坤路 632 号福州博物馆（邮政编码：956237）。联系电话：65913628。电子邮箱：ohkyi@lkifmehz.museums.cn

Zhù zhǐ: Nìng Jū Chuí Fújiàn Shěng Fúzhōu Shì Zhǎnglè Qū Lěi Kūn Lù 632 Hào Fúzōu Bó Wù Guǎn (Yóuzhèng Biānmǎ：956237). Liánxì Diànhuà：65913628. Diànzǐ Yóuxiāng：ohkyi@lkifmehz.museums.cn

Ju Chui Ning, Fuzhou Museum, 632 Lei Kun Road, Changle District, Fuzhou, Fujian. Postal Code: 956237. Phone Number：65913628. E-mail：ohkyi@lkifmehz.museums.cn

715。姓名: 东门炯坡

住址（大学）：福建省南平市光泽县岐福大学仲勇路 988 号（邮政编码：631915）。联系电话：58340018。电子邮箱：xpfyl@lqvwyndj.edu.cn

Zhù zhǐ: Dōngmén Jiǒng Pō Fújiàn Shěng Nánpíng Shì Guāngzé Xiàn Qí Fú DàxuéZhòng Yǒng Lù 988 Hào (Yóuzhèng Biānmǎ：631915). Liánxì Diànhuà：58340018. Diànzǐ Yóuxiāng：xpfyl@lqvwyndj.edu.cn

Jiong Po Dongmen, Qi Fu University, 988 Zhong Yong Road, Guangze County, Nanping, Fujian. Postal Code: 631915. Phone Number：58340018. E-mail：xpfyl@lqvwyndj.edu.cn

716。姓名: 井坤守

住址（机场）：福建省南平市建阳区甫王路 925 号南平磊帆国际机场（邮政编码：416903）。联系电话：90254585。电子邮箱：smnza@fvoxiquw.airports.cn

Zhù zhǐ: Jǐng Kūn Shǒu Fújiàn Shěng Nánpíng Shì Jiàn Yáng Qū Fǔ Wáng Lù 925 Hào Nánpíng Lěi Fān Guó Jì Jī Chǎng（Yóuzhèng Biānmǎ：416903). Liánxì Diànhuà：90254585. Diànzǐ Yóuxiāng：smnza@fvoxiquw.airports.cn

Kun Shou Jing, Nanping Lei Fan International Airport, 925 Fu Wang Road, Jianyang District, Nanping, Fujian. Postal Code: 416903. Phone Number：90254585. E-mail：smnza@fvoxiquw.airports.cn

717。姓名: 年译钢

住址（公园）：福建省福州市晋安区彬译路 953 号员伦公园（邮政编码：534312）。联系电话：36933660。电子邮箱：hwmjb@beiwxduj.parks.cn

Zhù zhǐ: Nián Yì Gāng Fújiàn Shěng Fúzhōu Shì Jìn Ān Qū Bīn Yì Lù 953 Hào Yuán Lún Gōng Yuán（Yóuzhèng Biānmǎ：534312). Liánxì Diànhuà：36933660. Diànzǐ Yóuxiāng：hwmjb@beiwxduj.parks.cn

Yi Gang Nian, Yuan Lun Park, 953 Bin Yi Road, Jinan District, Fuzhou, Fujian. Postal Code: 534312. Phone Number：36933660. E-mail：hwmjb@beiwxduj.parks.cn

718。姓名: 蒯龙禹

住址（酒店）：福建省厦门市海沧区惟亚路 247 号领立酒店（邮政编码：899963）。联系电话：81028613。电子邮箱：yxecm@qktxrbhw.biz.cn

Zhù zhǐ: Kuǎi Lóng Yǔ Fújiàn Shěng Xiàmén Shì Hǎi Cāng Qū Wéi Yà Lù 247 Hào Lǐng Lì Jiǔ Diàn（Yóuzhèng Biānmǎ：899963). Liánxì Diànhuà：81028613. Diànzǐ Yóuxiāng：yxecm@qktxrbhw.biz.cn

Long Yu Kuai, Ling Li Hotel, 247 Wei Ya Road, Haicang District, Xiamen, Fujian. Postal Code: 899963. Phone Number：81028613. E-mail：yxecm@qktxrbhw.biz.cn

719。姓名: 连宝臻

住址（广场）: 福建省宁德市古田县智盛路 884 号恩继广场（邮政编码: 854093）。联系电话：87404841。电子邮箱：qnjrd@avnwiohk.squares.cn

Zhù zhǐ: Lián Bǎo Zhēn Fújiàn Shěng Níngdé Shì Gǔtián Xiàn Zhì Shèng Lù 884 Hào Ēn Jì Guǎng Chǎng（Yóuzhèng Biānmǎ：854093). Liánxì Diànhuà：87404841. Diànzǐ Yóuxiāng：qnjrd@avnwiohk.squares.cn

Bao Zhen Lian, En Ji Square, 884 Zhi Sheng Road, Gutian County, Ningde, Fujian. Postal Code: 854093. Phone Number：87404841. E-mail：qnjrd@avnwiohk.squares.cn

720。姓名: 皮彬近

住址（湖泊）: 福建省泉州市洛江区超翼路 777 号阳乐湖（邮政编码: 356926）。联系电话：41537960。电子邮箱：ounjw@jaefidmo.lakes.cn

Zhù zhǐ: Pí Bīn Jìn Fújiàn Shěng Quánzhōu Shì Luò Jiāng Qū Chāo Yì Lù 777 Hào Yáng Lè Hú（Yóuzhèng Biānmǎ：356926). Liánxì Diànhuà：41537960. Diànzǐ Yóuxiāng：ounjw@jaefidmo.lakes.cn

Bin Jin Pi, Yang Le Lake, 777 Chao Yi Road, Luojiang District, Quanzhou, Fujian. Postal Code: 356926. Phone Number：41537960. E-mail：ounjw@jaefidmo.lakes.cn

CHAPTER 5: NAME, SURNAME & ADDRESSES (121-150)

721。姓名: 高源翼

住址（寺庙）：福建省莆田市荔城区威陆路 574 号自食寺（邮政编码：478327）。联系电话：68353029。电子邮箱：gujxh@pwsrjhlz.god.cn

Zhù zhǐ: Gāo Yuán Yì Fújiàn Shěng Pútián Shì Lì Chéngqū Wēi Lù Lù 574 Hào Zì Shí Sì (Yóuzhèng Biānmǎ: 478327). Liánxì Diànhuà: 68353029. Diànzǐ Yóuxiāng: gujxh@pwsrjhlz.god.cn

Yuan Yi Gao, Zi Shi Temple, 574 Wei Lu Road, Licheng District, Putian, Fujian. Postal Code: 478327. Phone Number: 68353029. E-mail: gujxh@pwsrjhlz.god.cn

722。姓名: 宋化迅

住址（广场）：福建省漳州市南靖县世民路 153 号独亮广场（邮政编码：906407）。联系电话：15193359。电子邮箱：bcmgz@wdxsqmpo.squares.cn

Zhù zhǐ: Sòng Huà Xùn Fújiàn Shěng Zhāngzhōu Shì Nán Jìng Xiàn Shì Mín Lù 153 Hào Dú Liàng Guǎng Chǎng (Yóuzhèng Biānmǎ: 906407). Liánxì Diànhuà: 15193359. Diànzǐ Yóuxiāng: bcmgz@wdxsqmpo.squares.cn

Hua Xun Song, Du Liang Square, 153 Shi Min Road, Nanjing County, Zhangzhou, Fujian. Postal Code: 906407. Phone Number: 15193359. E-mail: bcmgz@wdxsqmpo.squares.cn

723。姓名: 蒯源立

住址（公共汽车站）：福建省漳州市华安县盛可路 558 号人惟站（邮政编码：957852）。联系电话：43298305。电子邮箱：wvkol@zdkvcelu.transport.cn

Zhù zhǐ: Kuǎi Yuán Lì Fújiàn Shěng Zhāngzhōu Shì Huáānxiàn Shèng Kě Lù 558 Hào Rén Wéi Zhàn (Yóuzhèng Biānmǎ: 957852). Liánxì Diànhuà: 43298305. Diànzǐ Yóuxiāng: wvkol@zdkvcelu.transport.cn

Yuan Li Kuai, Ren Wei Bus Station, 558 Sheng Ke Road, Huaan County, Zhangzhou, Fujian. Postal Code: 957852. Phone Number：43298305. E-mail：wvkol@zdkvcelu.transport.cn

724。姓名: 耿智茂

住址（机场）：福建省平潭综合实验区平潭县庆尚路 660 号平潭综合实验区隆亮国际机场（邮政编码：454847）。联系电话：29643822。电子邮箱：hlamo@yhfgtopb.airports.cn

Zhù zhǐ: Gěng Zhì Mào Fújiàn Shěng Píng Tán Zònghé Shíyàn Qū Píng Tán Xiàn Qìng Shàng Lù 660 Hào Píng Tán Zòngé íyàn Qū Lóng Liàng Guó Jì Jī Chǎng (Yóuzhèng Biānmǎ：454847). Liánxì Diànhuà：29643822. Diànzǐ Yóuxiāng：hlamo@yhfgtopb.airports.cn

Zhi Mao Geng, Pingtan Comprehensive Experimental Area Long Liang International Airport, 660 Qing Shang Road, Pingtan County, Pingtan Comprehensive Experimental Area, Fujian. Postal Code: 454847. Phone Number：29643822. E-mail：hlamo@yhfgtopb.airports.cn

725。姓名: 司马石智

住址（博物院）：福建省福州市晋安区九愈路 336 号福州博物馆（邮政编码：552682）。联系电话：82123212。电子邮箱：xpgew@pldfxctv.museums.cn

Zhù zhǐ: Sīmǎ Dàn Zhì Fújiàn Shěng Fúzhōu Shì Jìn Ān Qū Jiǔ Yù Lù 336 Hào Fúzōu Bó Wù Guǎn (Yóuzhèng Biānmǎ：552682). Liánxì Diànhuà：82123212. Diànzǐ Yóuxiāng：xpgew@pldfxctv.museums.cn

Dan Zhi Sima, Fuzhou Museum, 336 Jiu Yu Road, Jinan District, Fuzhou, Fujian. Postal Code: 552682. Phone Number：82123212. E-mail：xpgew@pldfxctv.museums.cn

726。姓名: 古汉祥

住址（湖泊）：福建省南平市光泽县晗谢路 848 号淹乐湖 （邮政编码：761881）。联系电话：79441156。电子邮箱：qtxwk@ydrplhmv.lakes.cn

Zhù zhǐ: Gǔ Hàn Xiáng Fújiàn Shěng Nánpíng Shì Guāngzé Xiàn Hán Xiè Lù 848 Hào Yān Lè Hú （Yóuzhèng Biānmǎ：761881). Liánxì Diànhuà：79441156. Diànzǐ Yóuxiāng：qtxwk@ydrplhmv.lakes.cn

Han Xiang Gu, Yan Le Lake, 848 Han Xie Road, Guangze County, Nanping, Fujian. Postal Code: 761881. Phone Number：79441156. E-mail：qtxwk@ydrplhmv.lakes.cn

727。姓名: 后惟世

住址（医院）：福建省厦门市同安区珂铁路 627 号铁译医院 （邮政编码：154692）。联系电话：68446622。电子邮箱：ntlzf@gumzkcsl.health.cn

Zhù zhǐ: Hòu Wéi Shì Fújiàn Shěng Xiàmén Shì Tóngān Qū Kē Tiě Lù 627 Hào Fū Yì Yī Yuàn （Yóuzhèng Biānmǎ：154692). Liánxì Diànhuà：68446622. Diànzǐ Yóuxiāng：ntlzf@gumzkcsl.health.cn

Wei Shi Hou, Fu Yi Hospital, 627 Ke Tie Road, Tongan District, Xiamen, Fujian. Postal Code: 154692. Phone Number：68446622. E-mail：ntlzf@gumzkcsl.health.cn

728。姓名: 鞠盛土

住址（酒店）：福建省三明市宁化县勇冠路 517 号焯大酒店 （邮政编码：249529）。联系电话：71652066。电子邮箱：ecrnt@abhxgroj.biz.cn

Zhù zhǐ: Jū Chéng Tǔ Fújiàn Shěng Sānmíng Shì Níng Huà Xiàn Yǒng Guàn Lù 517 Hào Zhuō Dài Jiǔ Diàn （Yóuzhèng Biānmǎ：249529). Liánxì Diànhuà：71652066. Diànzǐ Yóuxiāng：ecrnt@abhxgroj.biz.cn

Cheng Tu Ju, Zhuo Dai Hotel, 517 Yong Guan Road, Ninghua County, Sanming, Fujian. Postal Code: 249529. Phone Number：71652066. E-mail：ecrnt@abhxgroj.biz.cn

729。姓名：笪征翼

住址（火车站）：福建省三明市泰宁县昌胜路 133 号三明站（邮政编码：778813）。联系电话：73715416。电子邮箱：yfdha@sdyroelj.chr.cn

Zhù zhǐ: Dá Zhēng Yì Fújiàn Shěng Sānmíng Shì Tài Níngxiàn Chāng Shèng Lù 133 Hào ānmíng Zhàn（Yóuzhèng Biānmǎ：778813). Liánxì Diànhuà：73715416. Diànzǐ Yóuxiāng：yfdha@sdyroelj.chr.cn

Zheng Yi Da, Sanming Railway Station, 133 Chang Sheng Road, Taining County, Sanming, Fujian. Postal Code: 778813. Phone Number：73715416. E-mail：yfdha@sdyroelj.chr.cn

730。姓名：利强友

住址（医院）：福建省厦门市思明区亭福路 639 号勇胜医院（邮政编码：649595）。联系电话：22592589。电子邮箱：dzvso@pzrymqku.health.cn

Zhù zhǐ: Lì Qiǎng Yǒu Fújiàn Shěng Xiàmén Shì Sī Míng Qū Tíng Fú Lù 639 Hào Yǒng Shēng Yī Yuàn（Yóuzhèng Biānmǎ：649595). Liánxì Diànhuà：22592589. Diànzǐ Yóuxiāng：dzvso@pzrymqku.health.cn

Qiang You Li, Yong Sheng Hospital, 639 Ting Fu Road, Siming District, Xiamen, Fujian. Postal Code: 649595. Phone Number：22592589. E-mail：dzvso@pzrymqku.health.cn

731。姓名：夏维化

住址（大学）：福建省三明市沙县区鸣石大学尚辉路 342 号（邮政编码：308652）。联系电话：39234572。电子邮箱：qaifr@tzyswopg.edu.cn

Zhù zhǐ: Xià Wéi Huà Fújiàn Shěng Sānmíng Shì Shāxiàn Qū Míng Shí DàxuéShàng Huī Lù 342 Hào（Yóuzhèng Biānmǎ：308652). Liánxì Diànhuà：39234572. Diànzǐ Yóuxiāng：qaifr@tzyswopg.edu.cn

Wei Hua Xia, Ming Shi University, 342 Shang Hui Road, Shaxian District, Sanming, Fujian. Postal Code: 308652. Phone Number：39234572. E-mail：qaifr@tzyswopg.edu.cn

732。姓名：杜兵昌

住址（湖泊）：福建省南平市武夷山市桥坡路 237 号甫民湖（邮政编码：620345）。联系电话：94399832。电子邮箱：otema@xfqheyzr.lakes.cn

Zhù zhǐ: Dù Bīng Chāng Fújiàn Shěng Nánpíng Shì Wǔyíshān Shì Qiáo Pō Lù 237 Hào Fǔ Mín Hú（Yóuzhèng Biānmǎ：620345). Liánxì Diànhuà：94399832. Diànzǐ Yóuxiāng：otema@xfqheyzr.lakes.cn

Bing Chang Du, Fu Min Lake, 237 Qiao Po Road, Wuyishan City, Nanping, Fujian. Postal Code: 620345. Phone Number：94399832. E-mail：otema@xfqheyzr.lakes.cn

733。姓名：邹大食

住址（火车站）：福建省平潭综合实验区平潭县全胜路 652 号平潭综合实验区站（邮政编码：667104）。联系电话：52610652。电子邮箱：fgiqo@pdikorgu.chr.cn

Zhù zhǐ: Zōu Dài Shí Fújiàn Shěng Píng Tán Zònghé Shíyàn Qū Píng Tán Xiàn Quán Shēng Lù 652 Hào Píng Tán Zòngé íyàn Qū Zhàn（Yóuzhèng Biānmǎ：667104). Liánxì Diànhuà：52610652. Diànzǐ Yóuxiāng：fgiqo@pdikorgu.chr.cn

Dai Shi Zou, Pingtan Comprehensive Experimental Area Railway Station, 652 Quan Sheng Road, Pingtan County, Pingtan Comprehensive Experimental Area, Fujian. Postal Code: 667104. Phone Number：52610652. E-mail：fgiqo@pdikorgu.chr.cn

734。姓名：俞秀国

住址（寺庙）：福建省漳州市漳浦县桥宝路 811 号独强寺（邮政编码：538519）。联系电话：47057559。电子邮箱：okhaw@uytlojrm.god.cn

Zhù zhǐ: Yú Xiù Guó Fújiàn Shěng Zhāngzhōu Shì Zhāng Pǔ Xiàn Qiáo Bǎo Lù 811 Hào Dú Qiáng Sì (Yóuzhèng Biānmǎ: 538519). Liánxì Diànhuà: 47057559. Diànzǐ Yóuxiāng: okhaw@uytlojrm.god.cn

Xiu Guo Yu, Du Qiang Temple, 811 Qiao Bao Road, Zhangpu County, Zhangzhou, Fujian. Postal Code: 538519. Phone Number: 47057559. E-mail: okhaw@uytlojrm.god.cn

735。姓名: 曲大伦

住址（火车站）：福建省福州市鼓楼区原翰路 957 号福州站（邮政编码：871691）。联系电话：89259347。电子邮箱：noqpe@ybimlekj.chr.cn

Zhù zhǐ: Qū Dà Lún Fújiàn Shěng Fúzhōu Shì Gǔlóu Qū Yuán Hàn Lù 957 Hào Fúzōu Zhàn (Yóuzhèng Biānmǎ: 871691). Liánxì Diànhuà: 89259347. Diànzǐ Yóuxiāng: noqpe@ybimlekj.chr.cn

Da Lun Qu, Fuzhou Railway Station, 957 Yuan Han Road, Gulou District, Fuzhou, Fujian. Postal Code: 871691. Phone Number: 89259347. E-mail: noqpe@ybimlekj.chr.cn

736。姓名: 钦洵臻

住址（博物院）：福建省厦门市集美区亮超路 742 号厦门博物馆（邮政编码：784382）。联系电话：78109673。电子邮箱：ilksr@jaoympqc.museums.cn

Zhù zhǐ: Qīn Xún Zhēn Fújiàn Shěng Xiàmén Shì Jíměi Qū Liàng Chāo Lù 742 Hào Xiàmén Bó Wù Guǎn (Yóuzhèng Biānmǎ: 784382). Liánxì Diànhuà: 78109673. Diànzǐ Yóuxiāng: ilksr@jaoympqc.museums.cn

Xun Zhen Qin, Xiamen Museum, 742 Liang Chao Road, Jimei District, Xiamen, Fujian. Postal Code: 784382. Phone Number: 78109673. E-mail: ilksr@jaoympqc.museums.cn

737。姓名: 娄员陶

住址（大学）：福建省厦门市集美区祥熔大学郁岐路 829 号（邮政编码：533358）。联系电话：37859383。电子邮箱：puasv@odeyjanz.edu.cn

Zhù zhǐ: Lóu Yún Táo Fújiàn Shěng Xiàmén Shì Jíměi Qū Xiáng Róng DàxuéYù Qí Lù 829 Hào (Yóuzhèng Biānmǎ：533358). Liánxì Diànhuà：37859383. Diànzǐ Yóuxiāng：puasv@odeyjanz.edu.cn

Yun Tao Lou, Xiang Rong University, 829 Yu Qi Road, Jimei District, Xiamen, Fujian. Postal Code: 533358. Phone Number：37859383. E-mail：puasv@odeyjanz.edu.cn

738。姓名: 苍熔阳

住址（火车站）：福建省漳州市平和县淹钢路 998 号漳州站（邮政编码：205754）。联系电话：39788268。电子邮箱：jpwdn@mtuiadwf.chr.cn

Zhù zhǐ: Cāng Róng Yáng Fújiàn Shěng Zhāngzhōu Shì Pínghé Xiàn Yān Gāng Lù 998 Hào Zāngzōu Zhàn (Yóuzhèng Biānmǎ：205754). Liánxì Diànhuà：39788268. Diànzǐ Yóuxiāng：jpwdn@mtuiadwf.chr.cn

Rong Yang Cang, Zhangzhou Railway Station, 998 Yan Gang Road, Pinghe County, Zhangzhou, Fujian. Postal Code: 205754. Phone Number：39788268. E-mail：jpwdn@mtuiadwf.chr.cn

739。姓名: 都轼己

住址（机场）：福建省漳州市龙海区坚员路 628 号漳州晖祥国际机场（邮政编码：814522）。联系电话：85458696。电子邮箱：segdf@whpabtdn.airports.cn

Zhù zhǐ: Dū Shì Jǐ Fújiàn Shěng Zhāngzhōu Shì Lóng Hǎiqū Jiān Yuán Lù 628 Hào Zāngzōu Huī Xiáng Guó Jì Jī Chǎng (Yóuzhèng Biānmǎ：814522). Liánxì Diànhuà：85458696. Diànzǐ Yóuxiāng：segdf@whpabtdn.airports.cn

Shi Ji Du, Zhangzhou Hui Xiang International Airport, 628 Jian Yuan Road, Longhai District, Zhangzhou, Fujian. Postal Code: 814522. Phone Number：85458696. E-mail：segdf@whpabtdn.airports.cn

740。姓名: 夹谷坡学

住址（博物院）：福建省泉州市洛江区近焯路 546 号泉州博物馆（邮政编码：792213）。联系电话：39104899。电子邮箱：putfm@ptsegyvz.museums.cn

Zhù zhǐ: Jiágǔ Pō Xué Fújiàn Shěng Quánzhōu Shì Luò Jiāng Qū Jìn Chāo Lù 546 Hào Quánzōu Bó Wù Guǎn （Yóuzhèng Biānmǎ：792213). Liánxì Diànhuà：39104899. Diànzǐ Yóuxiāng：putfm@ptsegyvz.museums.cn

Po Xue Jiagu, Quanzhou Museum, 546 Jin Chao Road, Luojiang District, Quanzhou, Fujian. Postal Code: 792213. Phone Number：39104899. E-mail：putfm@ptsegyvz.museums.cn

741。姓名: 陈谢轼

住址（家庭）：福建省莆田市荔城区近舟路 241 号翰斌公寓 38 层 287 室（邮政编码：638219）。联系电话：29719366。电子邮箱：xcyfv@zcbmdflv.cn

Zhù zhǐ: Chén Xiè Shì Fújiàn Shěng Pútián Shì Lì Chéngqū Jìn Zhōu Lù 241 Hào Hàn Bīn Gōng Yù 38 Céng 287 Shì (Yóuzhèng Biānmǎ：638219). Liánxì Diànhuà：29719366. Diànzǐ Yóuxiāng：xcyfv@zcbmdflv.cn

Xie Shi Chen, Room# 287, Floor# 38, Han Bin Apartment, 241 Jin Zhou Road, Licheng District, Putian, Fujian. Postal Code: 638219. Phone Number：29719366. E-mail：xcyfv@zcbmdflv.cn

742。姓名: 元红智

住址（机场）：福建省泉州市德化县盛锤路 867 号泉州敬乐国际机场（邮政编码：986640）。联系电话：32023240。电子邮箱：qkmba@ydlspiar.airports.cn

Zhù zhǐ: Yuán Hóng Zhì Fújiàn Shěng Quánzhōu Shì Dé Huà Xiàn Shèng Chuí Lù 867 Hào Quánzōu Jìng Lè Guó Jì Jī Chǎng（Yóuzhèng Biānmǎ：986640）. Liánxì Diànhuà：32023240. Diànzǐ Yóuxiāng：qkmba@ydlspiar.airports.cn

Hong Zhi Yuan, Quanzhou Jing Le International Airport, 867 Sheng Chui Road, Dehua County, Quanzhou, Fujian. Postal Code: 986640. Phone Number：32023240. E-mail：qkmba@ydlspiar.airports.cn

743。姓名: 公孙际食

住址（寺庙）：福建省福州市台江区葛跃路 190 号领成寺（邮政编码：578294）。联系电话：82525411。电子邮箱：cpvai@zkmeywtr.god.cn

Zhù zhǐ: Gōngsūn Jì Yì Fújiàn Shěng Fúzhōu Shì Tái Jiāng Qū Gé Yuè Lù 190 Hào Lǐng Chéng Sì（Yóuzhèng Biānmǎ：578294）. Liánxì Diànhuà：82525411. Diànzǐ Yóuxiāng：cpvai@zkmeywtr.god.cn

Ji Yi Gongsun, Ling Cheng Temple, 190 Ge Yue Road, Taijiang District, Fuzhou, Fujian. Postal Code: 578294. Phone Number：82525411. E-mail：cpvai@zkmeywtr.god.cn

744。姓名: 夹谷鸣豪

住址（大学）：福建省龙岩市武平县轼胜大学水员路 482 号（邮政编码：408551）。联系电话：13639109。电子邮箱：xbmud@dnzxfctl.edu.cn

Zhù zhǐ: Jiágǔ Míng Háo Fújiàn Shěng Lóngyán Shì Wǔpíng Xiàn Shì Shēng DàxuéShuǐ Yuán Lù 482 Hào（Yóuzhèng Biānmǎ：408551）. Liánxì Diànhuà：13639109. Diànzǐ Yóuxiāng：xbmud@dnzxfctl.edu.cn

Ming Hao Jiagu, Shi Sheng University, 482 Shui Yuan Road, Wuping County, Longyan, Fujian. Postal Code: 408551. Phone Number：13639109. E-mail：xbmud@dnzxfctl.edu.cn

745。姓名: 祝迅征

住址（机场）：福建省平潭综合实验区平潭县盛阳路 752 号平潭综合实验区波寰国际机场（邮政编码：794590）。联系电话：69514415。电子邮箱：uyzmv@izthvqan.airports.cn

Zhù zhǐ: Zhù Xùn Zhēng Fújiàn Shěng Píng Tán Zònghé Shíyàn Qū Píng Tán Xiàn Shèng Yáng Lù 752 Hào Píng Tán Zòngé íyàn Qū Bō Huán Guó Jì Jī Chǎng (Yóuzhèng Biānmǎ：794590). Liánxì Diànhuà：69514415. Diànzǐ Yóuxiāng：uyzmv@izthvqan.airports.cn

Xun Zheng Zhu, Pingtan Comprehensive Experimental Area Bo Huan International Airport, 752 Sheng Yang Road, Pingtan County, Pingtan Comprehensive Experimental Area, Fujian. Postal Code: 794590. Phone Number：69514415. E-mail：uyzmv@izthvqan.airports.cn

746。姓名: 沙澜腾

住址（机场）：福建省漳州市南靖县振乐路 889 号漳州红秀国际机场（邮政编码：617830）。联系电话：71461943。电子邮箱：xavze@zwcpgvqa.airports.cn

Zhù zhǐ: Shā Lán Téng Fújiàn Shěng Zhāngzhōu Shì Nán Jìng Xiàn Zhèn Lè Lù 889 Hào Zāngzōu Hóng Xiù Guó Jì Jī Chǎng (Yóuzhèng Biānmǎ：617830). Liánxì Diànhuà：71461943. Diànzǐ Yóuxiāng：xavze@zwcpgvqa.airports.cn

Lan Teng Sha, Zhangzhou Hong Xiu International Airport, 889 Zhen Le Road, Nanjing County, Zhangzhou, Fujian. Postal Code: 617830. Phone Number：71461943. E-mail：xavze@zwcpgvqa.airports.cn

747。姓名: 包食学

住址（大学）：福建省南平市武夷山市顺启大学葛铁路 267 号（邮政编码：767565）。联系电话：12278282。电子邮箱：syqwn@pometnqd.edu.cn

Zhù zhǐ: Bāo Shí Xué Fújiàn Shěng Nánpíng Shì Wǔyíshān Shì Shùn Qǐ DàxuéGé Tiě Lù 267 Hào (Yóuzhèng Biānmǎ: 767565). Liánxì Diànhuà: 12278282. Diànzǐ Yóuxiāng: syqwn@pometnqd.edu.cn

Shi Xue Bao, Shun Qi University, 267 Ge Tie Road, Wuyishan City, Nanping, Fujian. Postal Code: 767565. Phone Number: 12278282. E-mail: syqwn@pometnqd.edu.cn

748。姓名: 诸葛惟科

住址（家庭）：福建省宁德市福安市臻亮路 163 号豪顺公寓 5 层 603 室（邮政编码：233236）。联系电话：99507267。电子邮箱：adcwm@sagodkzm.cn

Zhù zhǐ: Zhūgě Wéi Kē Fújiàn Shěng Níngdé Shì Fúān Shì Zhēn Liàng Lù 163 Hào Háo Shùn Gōng Yù 5 Céng 603 Shì (Yóuzhèng Biānmǎ: 233236). Liánxì Diànhuà: 99507267. Diànzǐ Yóuxiāng: adcwm@sagodkzm.cn

Wei Ke Zhuge, Room# 603, Floor# 5, Hao Shun Apartment, 163 Zhen Liang Road, Fuan, Ningde, Fujian. Postal Code: 233236. Phone Number: 99507267. E-mail: adcwm@sagodkzm.cn

749。姓名: 吕红顺

住址（火车站）：福建省厦门市集美区进嘉路 646 号厦门站（邮政编码：311190）。联系电话：29711290。电子邮箱：spqym@rwkhzean.chr.cn

Zhù zhǐ: Lǚ Hóng Shùn Fújiàn Shěng Xiàmén Shì Jíměi Qū Jìn Jiā Lù 646 Hào Xiàmén Zhàn (Yóuzhèng Biānmǎ: 311190). Liánxì Diànhuà: 29711290. Diànzǐ Yóuxiāng: spqym@rwkhzean.chr.cn

Hong Shun Llv, Xiamen Railway Station, 646 Jin Jia Road, Jimei District, Xiamen, Fujian. Postal Code: 311190. Phone Number: 29711290. E-mail: spqym@rwkhzean.chr.cn

750。姓名: 苍坚辉

住址（公司）：福建省三明市将乐县洵秀路 153 号锡隆有限公司（邮政编码：868536）。联系电话：61467336。电子邮箱：klube@lgfdkzmu.biz.cn

Zhù zhǐ: Cāng Jiān Huī Fújiàn Shěng Sānmíng Shì Jiāng Lè Xiàn Xún Xiù Lù 153 Hào Xī Lóng Yǒuxiàn Gōngsī（Yóuzhèng Biānmǎ：868536）. Liánxì Diànhuà：61467336. Diànzǐ Yóuxiāng：klube@lgfdkzmu.biz.cn

Jian Hui Cang, Xi Long Corporation, 153 Xun Xiu Road, Jiangle County, Sanming, Fujian. Postal Code: 868536. Phone Number：61467336. E-mail：klube@lgfdkzmu.biz.cn

Milton Keynes UK
Ingram Content Group UK Ltd.
UKHW052100241123
433194UK00013B/725